D1083002

THIRTY YEARS OF POETRY

By

JUDSON JEROME

Collected Poems: 1949 - 1979

CEDAR ROCK PRESS

1121 Madeline
New Braunfels, TX 78130

All but a few of these poems have previously been published in the following
magazines: *Antioch Review, Approach, Atlantic Monthly, Beloit Poetry Journal, Best
Articles and Stories, Canadian Poetry Magazine, Cedar Rock, Change, Chicago Tribune,
Chicago Review, Coastlines, College English, Colorado Quarterly, Communitas, Compass,
Contact, Dasien, Dayton Daily News, Dimensions, Earthenware, Epoch, Epos, ETC,
Firebird, Folio, The Green Revolution, Harper's, A Houyhnhnm's Scrapbook, The
Humanist, LA, Ladies' Home Journal, Mademoiselle, Mad River Quarterly, Mele,
The Nation, New Mexico Quarterly, New Orleans Poetry Journal, Orange County
Illustrated, Patterns, Perspective, Poetry, Poetry Dial, Prairie Schooner, St.
Louis Post Dispatch, San Francisco Review, Saturday Review, Shenandoah, Southwest
Review, Sparrow, Tri-Quarterly, Views, Virginia Quarterly Review, Voices, Western
Review, Yale Review, Yankee, Zohar,* and others I cannot remember. Many have
also appeared in these collections: *Light in the West,* Golden Quill Press, 1962
(a selection of the Book Club for Poetry); *The Ocean's Warning to the Skin Diver
and Other Love Poems* (with etchings by Kathan Brown), Crown Point Press, 1964
(edition limited to 25 copies); *Serenade* (with ethings by Kathan Brown), Crown
Point Press, 1967 (edition limited to 20 copies); *The Village and other poems,*
Trunk Press, 1976; *Public Domain,* Trunk Press, 1977; *Myrtle Whimple's Sampler,*
Trunk Press, 1977. Some have appeared in anthologies including *Best Poems of
1963, Best Poems of 1966* (Borestone Mountain Poetry Awards), Pacific Books;
Reflections on a Gift of Watermelon Pickle . . . and Other Modern Verse, Scott
Foresman, 1966, *The Honey and the Gall,* MacMillan, 1967.

Library of Congress Catalog Card Number: 79-54319
ISBN 0-930024-12-5

My other books include:

The Poet and the Poem, Writer's Digest Books, editions 1963, 1974, 1979.

The Fell of Dark (novel), Houghton Mifflin, 1966.

Poetry: Premeditated Art, Houghton Mifflin, 1968.

Plays for an Imaginary Theater (verse drama and autobiography), University of
Illinois Press, 1970.

Culture Out of Anarchy: the Reconstruction of American Higher Learning, Herder
and Herder, 1971.

Families of Eden: Communes and the New Anarchism, Seabury Press, 1974.

I Never Saw . . . (poems for children), Albert Whitman, 1974.

Publishing Poetry, Cedar Rock Press, 1979.

TABLE OF CONTENTS

asterisks indicate poems I prefer

iv

COLLECTION AND SELECTION

Rarely does a poet have the opportunity extended to me by
David Yates and *Cedar Rock* to collect whatever he wishes from
thirty years of work and to arrange and present it as he pleases.
Such a project is a little different from the kind of "collected
works" of an author made up after he dies. For one thing, I hope
nobody interprets this book as a valediction. I want to get
these thirty years salted away so I can begin on the next and
the next. But even in doing that I encounter a responsibility
I am not sure I can quite meet. A collection is not a selection.
A collection implies that everything available is included--good,
bad, or indifferent. I often go to a collected works with as
much interest in the weak as in the strong material, for I am
attempting to understand the author or his age, and I can sometimes get better insights from failures than from successes. A
collection is a kind of historical record. When a living author
makes his own, the temptation to impose a postdated image on the
past is very strong.

I tried to resist that temptation by being more inclusive
than selective. Yet I have not put in everything available,
and I would like to discuss briefly some of the reasons why I
limited the book to the last thirty years--and, even then, did
not include all my published poems, let alone those in the desk
drawer morgue. In fact, I tried to give the book some of the
advantages (both to poet and reader) of a selection by starring
in the table of contents those poems I would have chosen if my
space had been limited. Moreover, I have distorted the historical
record by changing poems from the form in which they first appeared.
There is hardly a poem here in which I haven't changed something.
Most often I merely corrected spelling, punctuation or grammar,
but I sometimes changed words, phrases, lopped off (or added) lines
or stanzas, changed titles, introduced new line breaks, and so on.
I asked to prepare the master for photo-reproduction on my
typewriter, so all details of the final arrangement, including
the typos, are my responsibility. The final result is a book

which has some of the inclusiveness of historical record, modified
by the tidiness of a selection. Many of the poems here please
other readers a great deal more than they please me. I have
included a few which have yet to find a single reader besides
myself who thinks they are worth saving. Almost all of the
poems, though, have been published, which means at least that
they must have appealed to some editor at some time over the
last thirty years.

None but scholars and fanatics really want to read *everything*
a writer has written, but if there are any of those out there,
they may find what is not in this book in my collected papers
in the Boston University Memorial Library. While I cannot say,
as Alexander Pope did, "I lisped in numbers, for the numbers
came," it is true that my earliest poem (that I know of) is
metrical and rhymed. It is a poem to my mother, written when I
was about eight, and the only copy is in Boston. My first
published poem was in a literary magazine, *Red Earth,* about 1944,
written when I was sixteen, a freshman at the University of
Oklahoma. It is also metrical and rhymed.

I mention that to explain the largest body of my work
(all unpublished, all in Boston) which is unrepresented here:
my free verse, mostly written between the time I was eighteen
and twenty-one, before and after I was drafted, during my year
on Okinawa, and in the period when I entered the University of
Chicago and was courting Marty. We were married in 1948, and
that seemed to put an end to my flirtation with free verse.
I grew up in a family of people who loved poetry, but they thought,
as most people seem to who have not been educated out of the
opinion, that poetry is by definition metrical and probably rhymed.
But I was the first in my family to go to college, and there I
read "The Love Song of J. Alfred Prufrock" and

> in Just
> spring   when the world is mud-
> luscious the little
> lame balloonman
>
> whistles   far   and wee

and got several modern ideas about poetry: that anything goes,
that obscurity = quality, and that meter and rhyme are a drag.
Obviously I understood very little about the form of the poetry
of Eliot and Cummings--and subsequently have learned as much from
them as from Frost, Shakespeare, Yeats, Hopkins and others
about meter and rhyme. But you know how freshmen are.

There was a delay of a couple of months between the time I
got my draft notice and the date I finally had to report for
duty. Loafing around home and feeling useless, I took to writing
funny-looking poetry. It shocked my family. I loved shocking
my family. They didn't understand it. I loved not being understood. Behind it all, I was scared as hell of going into the
army with all those men. It wasn't the war I was scared of. It
was the soldiers. I think my free verse had something to do with
proving my manhood.

This story is continued in the brief introductions to each
of the five sections of the book. I will just add that I do
seem to have a thing about containers. The question of meter,
or measurement of lines, is the first thing I ask myself about
a poem--my own or anyone else's. Content--what a poem says--is
of primary importance, but I couldn't say anything at all if I
didn't know what form, what kind of box, I was going to put it in,
just as I couldn't think without English. To others that storage
problem doesn't seem to be such an obsession. When someone
comes into the house with a new purchase, I find myself wondering
where we're going to put it almost before I find out what it is.
I eat all kinds of strange fare for lunch to clean up leftovers,
not so much to save money as to liberate refrigerator boxes. I'm
not bragging about this: I just want to tell you that's the
kinda guy I'm.

I chose the historical arrangement so you could follow the
times as well as the poet. My records are not good--and sometimes
I have had to guess when a poem was written, though I remember
for most. I did not attempt to arrange the poems within the
sections chronologically but was guided by considerations of
theme, variety, and convenience. Marty, Sandy, and Janet (not

the one in the poem with that title!), here in our commune,
advised me and helped catch my bloopers. (Janet, especially,
is a demon of a copy-reader.) I left out perhaps ten per cent
of the poems published in magazines between 1955 and about 1965,
mostly because they were boring or repetitive of others which
are included. I don't know what makes young poets so production-
oriented. Any of us would be lucky if a half-dozen of our
poems were remembered after we are gone. It is only longer
narratives or dramas--*Paradise Lost* or *Hamlet*--which preserve
more than a handful of pages, even of the greatest poets. Who
reads poems, poems, poems, one after another? The problem is
finding the few you may want to come back to.

This volume and the verse dramas collected in *Plays for
an Imaginary Theater* (University of Illinois Press) make available
all my poetry from the past thirty years which I wish to save.
I am extremely grateful to *Cedar Rock*, and to the folks at Downhill
Farm who took up the slack while I holed up for a few weeks
with my typewriter, for making this book possible.

> *Downhill Farm*
> *Hancock, Maryland 21750*
> *June, 1979*

1949-1953

About 1949 I took a course in poetry with J. V. Cunningham at the University of Chicago. Cunningham had studied with Ivor Winters and represented what might be called the right wing of New Criticism. "If this were a course in elephants," he began, "we would have to know what an elephant is. What is poetry?" For an hour or so he listened to us thrash around with our moonlight-in-a-frog's-belly speculations. Then he said that so far as he was concerned poetry was metrical writing. If it were anything else besides that, he didn't know what it was. I was infuriated. It sounded like something my family might say. But in defiance, just to prove I could do so if I chose, I wrote and turned in to him "My Doubt Ranged Free." He copied it out anonymously on the blackboard and spent an hour analyzing its strengths and weaknesses.

I must have been converted. Never since have I wandered far from my iambic norm, and when I do, I feel the strain of artificiality. Iambic is home. I take off my dress clothes and slop around in slippers, at ease and free to keep my mind on what I am saying.

While I was at Chicago and then Ohio State University, working for advanced degrees, my poetry was academic in flavor. "Night Nurse" is a leftover from my free verse days before 1949. It used to be free but now is iambic. "The Jittery Gentle Squirrel" is a kind of declaration of independence. I had already been hired by Antioch College as an assistant professor of English and was entering the Ohio State library for one of the last times. I stopped to watch a squirrel scratch, then went in and wrote the poem in my carrel. To hell with Bunyan, Hobbes, Cavaliers and the rest. I had a job already. It was the first poem of mine to be published since I was sixteen. I keep it for sentimental reasons.

MY DOUBT RANGED FREE

My doubt upon the land ranged free. It fed
where others trusted and believed: a child
for lunch, a test tube, home, and church were piled
upon its dinner plate alive and dead,
for all was sham except my love and me.

The land was bare. My doubt was fat with pride,
and, ardent beast, it purred at my delight;
but, fond of praise, and whetted, vain of might,
it looked again. It was not satisfied
until it turned, consumed my love and me.

MUSICIAN TO HIS MISTRESS

A caged canary, sweet, is hardly apt
to let the bars confine his arching trills.
Should I, then, loving, labor to adapt
my feelings to the ordinary thrills?
And, say I should: Should tears, or what, compute
the regularities of scales? You ask
for numbers from a trembling throat or flute.
Is music but a reasonable task?

Oh, free am I? You mean I am freely bound
to echo like a tube, responding well
to instinct. Ha! What slaves have ever found
pleasure or freedom in *that* nervy hell?
These chords are wrung from turning of the stars.
The bird in love bites gilding from his bars.

INSOMNIAC RIVER

Deeply the water worries flinty knots
that rise like bad springs in its bed
and turn the troubled surface where it lies,
reflecting garbled visions of the skies.

This that the river sees--rippling shadows
of overhanging trees and sodden stars,
and lights of land that look like larger stars--
serves for its notion of its last perfection.

Mistaking shore for sky and sky for sea,
it carries piously the clear cold rain--
and if the mountains touched the sea it might
not hesitate like this upon the plain.

But now the silt, cut in the splash of days
back when the sun glanced through clear pools, scattered
on unreflecting foam, now dulls and weighs
the slowing stream and muddies its conviction.

Clogged as it is with life, and at the arch
of age, it views perfection with a chill
and laps against its wifely shore more gently,
fondly forgetting ways of fight and search.

And the slow turns lie peacefully across
oblivious fields, and water warm and brown
works through the earth to pleasure-loving roots
which share its wealth but cannot share its loss.

But when the fields are black, alone the river
gleams its obedience as it has before.
Clogged as it is with guilt, impatient, blocked,
the stream resents the stagnant, sleeping shore.

All night it snarls by branches, bristles cold
in the flat wind, swirls fitfully through old
obliquities as though to make them straight--
to find where seas their absolutes unfold.

TO THE CHIEF OF SINNERS

General Bunyan could not leave
the Center, for dispatches came
like missiles from below, above.
He could not act until reprieve
or clear damnation (all the same)
    thundered finally
    in the War of Love.

YOU HAVE DONE IT NOW STOP wired
the Tempter. *IS THIS TRUE OH LORD?*
GET BACK TO WORK STOP YES I LOVE THEE.
But John, hourly cautious, tired,
thought lines were crossed. Again he poured
    his heart into the night:
    KEEP THINKING OF ME.

NIGHT NURSE

. . . palms freeze to the damn bannister . . .
when I made my choice I might have guessed
the good old heart would give when all undressed . . .
the best was plucked, the rest not even seen . . .
I might have known the ones I loved would lean
upon me for safe sleeping through the night
then tuck me like a bedpan out of sight . . . .

had I thought I'd have seen how deeply sanity
has its piles in the quagmire of vanity . . .
how good works work lonely on the lonely soul . . .
just you wait, it's own reward and all
that crap will finally extirpate even
the want of credit or regard . . . were I
just aware that when they said to give
they really meant to share . . . or best, invest . . .
and that to give yourself entails the peril
of finding that you've but performed and now
are sterile . . . or perhaps it was said for men
and either at the altar or over the counter
women are supposed to barter . . . one
day I'll slip on the damned ice and bust
my head and that will be the sum . . . remember
when you've fed on the dust you gather they say
that's really not the end to it . . . yeah . . . when
you eventually have a bellyful of dirt
you turn into it . . . girls with fat ankles learn
oh learn that giving spills through a broken hour
glass and blows, that living never faileth . . .
that seeing darkly bestows a certain radiance
                    on the rose . . .

ISHMAEL TO AHAB

Aboard my wallowing coffin, humble, I
reject this cowardly gratitude. The gods
who spared me from your damning did so with
disdain. This other life is in the theater
of the last life, but closer now I see
the shallow drops and hear the hollow stage.
Small wonder this mock quarterdeck could not
your tread maintain.
                        The pale, phlegmatic sea
accepts without a hiss the sinking sun.
It vomited back the chips and me unharmed.
Somewhere the whale, with his scarred cloud of brow
bleeding no pain, conscription served, returns
to silent and to equal company,
and the cool crests that topple where we were,
no more oblivious than he. Your eyes
gape, and your body, fouled in hemp, compressed
by sea, is circling stiffly through the cold
and dark. In timeless insubordination
this wreck of you shows more of search
than of obedience in its gravitation.

  Enormously objective I can see
you have found more than you will find again.
In search of knowledge you have found an end
of knowing. Knowing, though, is not your call.
Conviction, even as you fall, misleads.
The soggy bottom, still this side of God,
like Moby Dick, is but a further wall.

  O fool, Ahab, and twice a hasty fool!
To strike at malice where it cannot be--
or, if the whale were conscious as you thought,

to strike for striking, strike to beg defeat!
O holy fools who give your minds to gods,
you savages and clergymen at odds,
all following Ahab in a fog of credence
with fevered praise, or fear, or curses shrill,
expect not nature's credit or retreat--
deaf is the strength of growing things, and still!

I followed you and served, with some dissent,
and swear that had there been a scientist
faced you across your quarterdeck with the rest,
that he would have joined Ahab in his quest;
though several of us thought you wrong, not one
preferred his rightness to your fiery sin.
There is a manly power in belief
that, comprehending, I could not quite share;
and yet I could not comprehend its pull--
for when you met your hell and I was saved,
I felt regret.
                        This other hell where I
am left rewards with no such woman's gift
as grace. It disregards, but if a man
be great, it turns, annoyed, and thanks him with
its hate.
                        Not even that. I know not that.
Asea in comprehension, I have none:
no creed of love or hate on which to build.
A moment's thought, and schools of Moby Dicks,
and Christs and countries, mistresses of mind,
suddenly naught.
                        Could I resign my rightness

and my strength to gods to whom they are
not worth the taking, or, like Ahab, thrust
my spear in any clear contention, then
lose scope, be damned to narrow ignorance,
in the closed world believe a fragment of truth,
fragment of nonsense, could I but do this . . .
did I not comprehend my very wish . . .
the glory of my chase would soon obscure
the failure of my voyage. No one fails
who, numb to truth, pursues to the last lowering
and, dying, can mistake his own blood spouting
for the whale's.
                    Now casual scud clouds
ride low before the wind, besmudged and tattered,
helpless they sail, and fail to fill the sky.
My coffin has no keel; by a dumb gull,
hiding his legs, crossing the moon, am I
mocked, with now foot and now skull at the bow.

AULD LANG SYNE

At bridge on New Years ladies sit
(it seems much gayer than to knit)
and make decisions with the tips
of fingers on their waxen lips
and hardly hear the distant crack
of one more year dropped from the pack.

TRAINING FLIGHT

From the bug knob at the tail
of a disarmed seventeen
I leave Okinawa lying
on a scrolled sea. Green

are the paddied hills, and combed,
set wet by a delicate hand.
Jeeps jerk and six-bys labor,
hard beetles lost in sand.

A tuft of dust discloses
some military spoil
to the south (marked off-limits
to economic toil.)

But north, a flooded field
of pinpoints planting rice
gleams like an eye beholding
our noisy, aerial vice.

But never mind. We climb
ten thousand feet. Recall
those scalloped hills? From here
there are no hills at all.

The green worm, purple-fringed,
that twists on that blank sea
has clearly no connection
with roar-bound, mask-nosed me.

This silver sheath is real,
stretching its quivering wings,
sustaining visible steel,
swilling invisible springs.

WINTER IN EDEN

A dream ago I stood in Paradise,
and my tendons hung upon me like the vines
that choke the trees with love in Paradise
and ply the earth with seeds and sticky wines.
Bright fruit hung in the garden, and bright leaves

lay nudely in the sunlight without stirring,
when Eve in silence watched uprising coils
and heard the tickling tongue in hushness whirring.
I would have moved, but tendons clung to me.
I would have spoken, but all voices there

were smothered in the feverish folds of silence.
I looked out coldly through the vines and air.
It bound her body with long scaling clasp
of muscle that could crease and overcome
Eve's flesh. I heard their whispered bargaining

like distant voices in a catacomb.
A grey wind turned grey undersides of leaves.
Eyes thinned. Skin roughened like a lake that felt
a summer storm's descending chill, and I
thrilled with an equal need of warmth and guilt.

NUDE, RECLINING

I see her like a beach beneath a moon,
a vinegar sea all muttering in her hollows
and vegetation lying like a hand
upon the sand that waits where nothing follows.

By dark and salt, far out, the sea-life squirms.
Fish hang and vibrate like electric feathers.
Possibly octopi or oysters gape.
Deeper, the sphincter jaws, pale in all weathers.

Sun-storing sand, infertile (except where dirt
has lodged at the mouths of streams), is heaped by wind
blown clean from the bone-bottomed flats, in valleys
soft, sagging; cupped here, and there fanned thin.

Inland the ragged radar palms scan backwards,
leaning away from the sea; tall grasses gather,
whistling, behind hills; sparrows in oleanders
chirp when the branch blows; quiet snakes
grow leather.

She lies: clean marqin, radiant, wind-clothed, barren
(except for those whisking crabs) beneath a moon.
I spill her through my fingers, warm my arms,
and, roots in sand, I wilt too soon, too soon.

WHO SADLY KNOW

"People in this age are not so apt to kill themselves."
                    Dryden, Sir Martin Mar-all

You would scuff through the violets
with jangly boots and turn up earth,
oh Cavaliers. Your thrusts of wit
or sword or self excite our mirth--
and excite also certain fears:

When you have stript the lady down
to what you understand for sure,
oh Cavaliers, when savage sight
has raped the hypocrite demure,
can you endure what then appears?

When you have bruised and bound the whore
with her soft back against the stake,
oh Cavaliers, who suffers more--
the nerveless flesh or nerveless rake
who cracks his wit about her ears?

Crumpled upon the floor are clothes
with artificial flowers torn,
oh Cavaliers, by you who know
the soil in which all blooms are born,
who sadly know, oh Cavaliers.

HOBBES AND THE GHOSTS

"The Fields which answer'd well the *Ancients Plow,*
Spent and out-worn return no *Harvest* now,"
writes Cowley to me, posturing in his cell,
that windy oracle who blows out dooms
he does not understand. He says:
"We break up *Tombs* with *Sacrilegious hands;*
      Old Rubbish we remove;
To walk in Ruines, like vain *Ghosts,* we love."

The moon above is not so pale in conquest
as we old men with wenches in our pay.
Ha! I cackle, too, in the poetic way:
    "Tho' I am now past ninety, and too old
    T'expect preferment in the court of Cupid
    And many winters made mee ev'n so cold
    I am become almost all over stupid . . . ."

        ghosts: *So stupid dangle, wit all spent*
                 and running down the thighs of Lent,
                 your wisdom lost in hairy tangle
                 with those who dared to see that will
                    was free
                 and that the circle was not squared.

                 We love you, Hobbes, our mangy bear
                 chained in the pit, with thinning hair
                 and thinning wit, but you have said
                 yourself that when the motions cease
                    the man is dead.

Old men are drowned. The moisture gathers where
there is no struggling: Feet and legs will swell

that once were sound, and water loosens flesh
around the waist and all around. The mind
remains. On skulls the flesh is thin. And still
it gathers numbers in . . . then tells
with withered tongue.
                    My mind has never fumbled
like my ancient hands: platonic hands, too old
for loving, blurring the gesture, frightening her
who loves me in the sunlight when I talk.
We walk our walk. She stands all dumb with life
while I am turning, deep in water toiling,
head alive with trim moustaches, points
of fire beneath my bushy head of ashes,
then puts away my hand as though it were
a wisp of hair that brushed her cheek, distraction
in a maiden's summer morning. Our last years
we hold the young ones by the ears. We want
too much--that they should listen to our talk
and bear our palsied touch.

>   *Observe the arid spout of the Leviathan and find*
>   *how matter rises pure as wraith from purer mind*
>   *or how your words may stroke a cheek more softly*
>   *than your hand, or why a lady may be kind . . .*

I pay her, true, for writing down my spite.
If she could only draw! You know, without
my drawings I can hardly think: I need
the solid demonstration, solid line,
and now am left with algebra like broth
sustaining toothless age. By God, Descartes,
with broken compass, folded paper rule,
could ring me now with vortices! His heart
and he are now in separate tombs.
                                    I lock

the door at night against the thieves and sing
and play a prick-song on my lute--for health--
and say that this may add a year or two.
The stealth is what I fear: to think, and not
to hear them coming on, too soon, and silent
through the rooms as though they were ideals--
formlessly turning, timeful, fearful wheels.
And though a year or so my voice withstands,
soon it must rasp to a stop with inner sands,
feeling a friction time can never feel.
Time whispers now beyond discerning, turns,
rolling us under like a wave or wheel--
and only time, and only turning, turning.

> *Our old bear is afraid when the dogs are dead*
> *of the barking which echoes around his head,*
> *of forgotten truths and returning boasts:*
> *the feminine bear is afraid of ghosts!*

"The year of the Armada, doubtful year,
My mother brought forth twins--myself and fear,"
and we have taught each other how to live
to ninety-two. My fear has made me Christian,
or made me seek, at any rate, salvation,
revealed that rulers, when they speak,
want us to turn the other cheek,
that life is granted to the meek,
that strength comes from evasion and submission.
But spirits bore me.

I flushed them from the bed
of Selden when he died. I laughed at Mersenne,
who would save my soul. One need not hide
from ghosts, but only thieves and things that are.
I run, quite true, but not so far I cannot

spin in the light, put out my chin, and dare,
and run again. Timidity improves
one's logic and his skill at standing
quite close to ghosts and even thieves.   I parry
Wallis with compass needle, stab him when
he weaves; Charles I wheedle; Bramhall falls
to counter-accusation.   Christ and fear
have saved my reputation.

> *But time is unawed.   Fraud,*
> *no more than a locked door,*
> *can baffle decay.   Pray,*
> *cringe,*
> *subvert all your flesh love,*
> *devote your malign core,*
> *and squander your sense*
> *for God's recompense,*
> *for the long love, and the dry.*

My appearance is misleading;
look, my tallow palms are bleeding.
What I was, I did not mean.
What I seemed, I never was.
Do farmers know whom they are feeding?

> *The lock will crumble: Cromwell died, and shapes*
> *reformed.   Authorities, you found in youth,*
> *are no more permanent than truth, and kings*
> *are fallible and whores diseased and day*
> *smoulders through the night and darkness hangs*
> *above the light.   Now faced with time you say*
> *you never meant, when making men of matter,*
> *never meant to leave them subject to decay.*

THE JITTERY GENTLE SQUIRREL . . .

. . . has no right to such a belly
as hangs on the sidewalk
while he cocks his hind leg
and scratches a flea like some
miniature dog with a spring broke.

Besides the creepy critter has
long bent black fingers
with no thumbs, and when he looks at you
sidewise, his mouth all pulled down,
saying *I'm Aloysius Something the Goddamned Third*
so don't pick on me don't pick on me . . .

HE doesn't think he's cute
and neither would you if he
were a rat which he almost is.

1954-1958

For the twenty years beginning in 1953 I was heavily involved with Antioch College. For the first two years I was still writing my doctoral dissertation, but I interrupted that one evening in 1954, in the basement of our home in Yellow Springs, Ohio, to write the "Kiamichi Sonnets," about a region in Oklahoma where I had spent some crucial times of my boyhood. *Poetry* accepted "Deer Hunt" from that series. That encouragement launched me into writing poetry seriously and voluminously and submitting my work to magazines. I sent out too much, digging out all the salvageable poetry I had written while in graduate school and constantly producing new work. All the poems I sent out were eventually accepted by one magazine or another--over a hundred in some thirty magazines by 1960. John Ciardi, poetry editor of *Saturday Review*, was especially helpful and responsive. We had begun to be a family: Michelle was born in 1954, Beth in 1956, Polly in 1959, and I was preoccupied with both the richness and limitations of domestic life and amorous adventure.

I wanted to enlarge the audience for poetry and the function of poetry in our culture. Most of my colleagues were scientists of one sort or another, and I wanted to reach them and their families. I was fed up with the literati, both as audience for and critics of poetry. I wanted to break out of the short, subjective lyric, out of obscurity and preciousness. I was trying verse essays, even essay-sonnets, satire, narratives, plays, humor, social commentary. I was living in the social climate Allen Ginsberg protested in *Howl,* and "The Muse and I" describes the poetic world I was facing. As poetry editor for *Antioch Review* I was facing it at close hand.

We took summer camping trips to Nova Scotia and Maine, but mostly worked at the competing jobs of professional advancement and child-rearing, homemaking, learning to be sophisticated, in Yellow Springs.

KIAMICHI SONNETS

Deer Hunt
Because the warden is a cousin, my
mountain friends hunt in summer, when the deer
cherish each rattler-ridden spring, and I
have waited hours by a pool in fear
that manhood would require I shoot, or that
the steady drip of the hill would dull my ear
to a snake whispering near the log I sat
upon, and listened to the yelping cheer
of dogs and men resounding ridge to ridge.

I flinched at every lonely rifle crack,
my knuckles whitening where I gripped the edge
of age and clung, like retching, sinking back,
then gripping once again the monstrous gun,
since I, to be a man, had taken one.

*Noodling**
Where Mountain Fork is wide as an avenue
above the falls I stood all stick-white-legged
in the green stream on slick stones, watching true
noodlers, who wade in shoes, whose hands are ragged
nets in the water reaching under rocky
cavities, catching the quick tense fish
(or sometimes snake or turtle), men soft-talking
above the water, cursing their silent wish.
I bent my own bone back just like the men
and felt my tight hand quake beneath the stream,
an eerie hesitation, grabbed, and then
cold muscle whipped my palm. Now nights I dream
of sinking fingers into unseen gills
in the green deeps of distant burnished hills.

grappling

Memory of Grey Fox
Coleman, the old goat, could knock a squirrel
out of a tree with a rock and catch more perch
on a plug than you could seine. I see him lurch-
ing through the brush with a seventy-year-old hurl
of the body like a hobbled rabbit, white
head bobbing with its tilted turkey feather
(he was a clown), his tattered sneakers right-
stepping by twigs, silent to earth, his leather
hands fending branches, leaving not a trace.
His was a race of berry-eaters, thorn-
endurers, pinchers-of-women, gaunt of face,
who drank belly-down from springs, whose sons were born
like water from the teeming, hanging hill
stretched naked where the heavens chose to spill.

The Sinew of Survival
The jack-oak, like an Indian, enjoys
its little water, yellows late if at all,
crooks coppery arms, sinks ropy roots, employs
such wry deceptions to delay the fall--
just like the girls. I took one rustling walk
across parched hills it seemed some seven miles
with a Cherokee whose gently pimpled frock
was blooming out of season. Led by smiles
and swimming hips, I found we were emerging
from secret, soft and golden woodlands to
a bald rock ledge along the river, verging
white in the sun and hot, in open view,
for she preferred these blistering, bruising rigors
to loving in the shade among the chiggers.

MARE IN SEASON

In Nova Scotia this mare (let me tell you)
leaped, Lord, how she flung herself twisting,
such a great thing in the air, while,
oblivious, an old horse trotted by
on the road pulling the varnished gig
of an old man.
          More than fence
denied her, more than flesh, as she threw
that loglike head on massive-muscled
neck, all four hooves flying
hung to four flying legs, her
rump like a boulder hurled, tail
like a frond streaming.
                 Oh that aerial
arch of mare, those pounds and pounds
of flat spanking meat and mostly
those eyes (jelly under bony brows),
white sparked with pounds of wanting,
nostrils flecked and wide, rubber
hanging lips drawn anguished back,
and her eyes reaching (soft, if you
could see them).
              She was severed, open
to the salt old air of Nova Scotia.

GULL AT PLAY

From the dune-crest I saw an idiot gull
bucking a squall on the fringe of a fretful sea,
awkward and suicidal, flapping for no good end,
fat, overcivilized, no windhover he,

but my heart stirred, for in my flapping jacket
I too had hurled myself for fun headlong
into a wind too big and had begun
to feel the cleansing chill. Who knows what fun

is any more? I remember pilgrims streaming
out of Boston to the sea, their autos heavy
with sacramental freight, their kleenex boxes,
innertubes and cameras, gazing, dreaming

of some salty absolution, bringing their young
to be blessed in the ceremony of the out-
of-doors. This Sunday morning sand-in-the-teeth
set has few libertines; they are devout,

wear hair shirts (blazing tropic blooms), submit
themselves like penitents to the salt and sun,
not to the exquisite, artful agonies, but
to discomfort crude and pure. Since I am one

of such a holy breed, I can explain
somewhat what moves the gull and me. Suppose
in your pale condition, ignorant of the soil,
your hands no longer agents of your brain,

you woke on a desert island in a jock-strap.
With no tool but a pocket-knife, you devise
a gimcrack the city makes in plastic, sells
for a dime back home. Just think how you would clap

your rediscovered hands in celebration.
Similarly, if in the granite State of Maine
by the clear cold sea you wrest some campfire comfort
from driftwood, scrubby spruce and rocks, or rain

cutting around a stretched tarp does not
quite penetrate, or if, at Fundy, where
the headlands loom all shaggy in the fog,
the coffee perks, and in your duffle a pair

of dry socks waits your weakening, you know
my recluse ecstasies. Even the beach crowd
enjoys a form of flagellation, not
to feel the pain, but to feel after each blow

some measure of relief. Of course no pleasure
is more phony, more a sign of civilization
past the crest--when we feel pressed brutally
to sensitize our faculties, to treasure

our crude things, a rusty nail in a grimy hand.
But the need lies deep. Life lives a self-willed test,
or else that gull, fighting the wind out there,
over the curling breakers, would welcome rest.

THE VIOLENCE

we struck straight up the bluff by dark and tilted
forward on our ankles pumping hard seeing the flash
of moon sometimes through branches but mostly filtered

all sight out except direct footfalls and crashed
through where the branches hung too low unspeaking
usually even when we rested breathing deliberately

and then pumped on and pumped and finally breaking
on a bright meadow heard the laborious panic of cattle
rattle of deer and felt a wave of the field's

heat roll upon us looked at the light-edged lake
back far below and at the round moon held
on a cloud crest and crossed in grass calves aching

to the heights swilling cool air and went again
now on a gorge lip growing brush now turning
down again legs flung before too fast and when

it seemed level up again over forgotten fences
across road ruts then through a ravine with water
and table rocks and into woods all black

and crisscrossed with fallen trees webbed with dark
whips crackling scratching and snapping wickedly
our sweating faces while our ankles turned

under us and we tumbled down unseen gullies
strewn with logs knowing we were lost we leaned
into the wood snare angrily snaking blindly

until an hour later when we broke upon
the path strung down steep along a creek canyon
leading to a field shoulder-high in hay and the road

twisting home under trees with a breeze soft on
our necks our thighs throbbing and our minds stilled
in sweat and violence and at long last satisfied

MAINE RAIN: BUSTINS ISLAND

It was light at five, the single sugar cloud
pink in the sky, the gulls creaking, the blue
bay ruffed by a dawn south wind. I read
three hours till babies woke and I was through.
That south wind fretted all morning, dimmed the pale
Maine sun, pushed in a fog. Now rain, at five,
spatters the still grey bay, streams from the eaves,
and I am soggier than I am alive.

A day for beer. A day for love--with no covers.
A day for burning kerosene all day,
weathering passively on a granite island
with all the other people "from away,"
and kept indoors, now, by the clumsy thunder
and thinking not a thought above a wonder.

MIDWESTERN BEAR DANCE

Most communities now have toilets, few diseases
or bandanas or skirts that swirl around the clumping
field-shoes. But theaters. Most towns have movie houses
and a display of frozen foods in the grocery

(still with a wood floor), since few have time
to cook. There never was much art except
utilitarian fiddling for a dance, or fitting
wood with a hand plane, honing a blade, repairing

broken leather--but now that discipline goes
to getting good mileage, the hand touch to tuning by
turning a delicate knob--such modern crafts.
I am not yearning. The old days may have been

all blood where now is brain; the peasant head,
rich with old saws and knowledge of the beasts
and seasons, undeviating like an ancient water
wheel and grinding corn into meal, was narrow

and creaking with its wooden fins. These shells
of towns (places you live) with technological
overlay are gentled and trained (bears taught to dance
on balls), pathetic, but crudely civilized.

I am not yearning. Nevertheless I am glad
on a June morning to see the old days manifested
still. You see aerials now between the steeples
and the tops of trees. The road signs say

a speed and warn you of unnamed electrical devices.
After the motels come the railroad tracks--
jarring remembrance of an era--a feed store,
some filling stations, long checker-windowed school,

all silent. The two-block stretch of boxlike stores
stirs like an animate accordian. That is where you see
the aprons--white and sanitary, delivered from
a sanitary laundry in the city

thirty miles away. A grocer, aproned, squints
at the sun and cranks down his awning. A baker's boy
fresh out of school, leaning with caved shoulders
against the store, hands in pockets under

his white apron, plots with a girl in shorts how young
ones can escape the town. These might be medieval
stalls, the aprons leather, the clapboard steeples
medieval spires for all the subterranean

change. The old bear dances as he must for food,
may even change his toilet habits, but beneath
his cocked straw hat there lies a bear brain, savage
and stupid as a bear's, but, in its bear-way, wise.

A BURNISHED THRONE

In a metal boat, gleaming, new,
with blue outboard motor to match,
all of which rig one would guess

cost a pretty penny and gets lifted
out of the water to avoid a scratch,
sits a family, father at the stern,

red at the neck and on the lower arms,
muttering that they have drifted
too close to the shore, a yellow-

headed son who must not scare
the fish, who may learn
about the motor and the craft

of leisure, and a pretty mother
dangling an impotent pole--
and, as the sociologists say,

each one plays a role.
What can the father do?
Swing out the screaming reel

and run the boat and in fcw
deep words keep order, educate
his son. His son may feel

the water with his fingers,
find a fly in the tackle box,
tell his mother to be still,

who sits, a queen, in sunglasses
and baseball cap, and at the bow will
comment on things on shore,

whether shushed or not, and begs
her subjects to turn the boat
so she may evenly tan her legs.

DECRESCENDO

At five the rain is gone and robins
hunt in yellow pools of sun like
fat two-footed spiders, rapid,
lame, and the green world is sodden
and subdued. Hardly a hint of the storm

stays: a twig blown down still bearing
leaves, long low ripples on the lake
from habit (the wind being dead), inside
the tent, residual fidgeting (business
with cigarets), but mostly staring

at the absence of the storm we stared at.

A STORM TIME

Last night here on Cape Breton winds
bearing a buckshot rain descended
off the highlands, flattened ten tents

on a bluff across the brook. They rocked
us in the car. The windows spat.
The surf outside rolled pebbles, boulders,

in its bony jaws. All you could see was
whirling spew of wet wind
tossing grass and light-splashed

instants of waves charging low
into the wind with shoulders bent
and faces full of froth, bellowing

as they laid into the rocks, breathing
hard. (I thought of desperate tight-
lunged men, at a shot dropping to knees

and scattering white arms of spray.)
All night this elemental curse,
this faceless sky. Today is grey,

clouds in a chilly boil, the waves
on the beach (ten in a minute) heave
themselves like fragments of a half-

remembered dream. We stopped by the shelter
where the evicted tenters stood,
all unfamiliar, shielding a hot

wood stove. Out front one sawed at a pump
handle, his jacket flying, wind whipping a stream from the pump spout.

The rest in damp clothes, waiting for
a sign of clearning weather: door-
leaners, eaters by ritual, chiders

of children, sodden, sociable hermits
far from their cities, each one piecing
together scraps of last night's squalling

horror, the banging of canvas, tangle
of rope, the drenching black, fingers
numb, fumbling with property, and long

night and now longer day by these massive
things: the round brown hills, wind, sea--
not hostile, friendly, or derisive,

rolling their regular rhythm, cold,
oblivious, but (how dreams hang on!)
at storm times seeming to take hold.

NINE TO ELEVEN

After six of us got a quart of gin
about half down and the first hand moved
for the cubes of cheese and ham and Polish
sausage, it was dark enough we missed

subtleties of faces there on the porch
(with the wind coming through lightly)
and talked in longer sentences, our
laughs meaning more now, and defining

of positions done: father, mother
daughter, son, my wife and I, all
old enough and ready enough after half
the bottle to forget that one was this,

the other that, maneuvering done,
the way clean before us (with the lake
lapping placidly, the trees just breathing)
and the way clean with still half a quart

of gin to help us coast to anonymity
(with, one said, a beautiful five-eighths moon
the only light, and *it* tolerant),
so only another hour, say, before

we were talking in shorter sentences, happily
bored, having felt one another through, and
one went to bed and five swam out
nude in the moonlight, and we were there.

PHEASANT PLUCKING . . .

. . . takes nerve to dip that autumn harmony
of feathers into boiling water, sink
fingers into the oilslick of his breast,
analyze the infinite eyes of his colors
making particles of fluff, to render
bare the orange skin
                    . . . takes quite a tug
to undo the tail's indolent arc, to make
a scrawny finger of what once was proud
as wing, to scatter hackles in the wind
until the bones and belly of the bird
protrude indecently
                    . . . but no offense
(except this of the knife) can humble him,
nude to the chin, a beauty all too bare,
blue-headed, firm of beak, vermillion stare.

NIGHT COMFORT

About two a mosquito or a thought
stabbed me to wakefulness. I caught
then the air of the morning, saw the clear
black shadows on the grass. A mere
mile out the window stood the moon,

pure as an heirloom plate. June
warmth, uncovering, left the dew.
(I smelled dew in the air, cool through
the indoor body-breath and heat).
Marty woke when I pulled the sheet

up, so we smoked--batting now and then
at bugs and words. Sticky. But when
one thought of moving it seemed a pleasure
to be sticky, and, well, stink. One measure
of happiness is such consolation

with the real. However, limitation
made bladders radical, soon brought
unrest. Once up we whimsically sought
the other comfort, that of the lie.
So as not to wake the baby, I

led us by matchlight to the door,
and we creaked out, nude to the core,
under the ivory moon where soft
damp grass chilled us. Then we doffed
such indoor prose as chills. The black

lake lay like a film to be thrown back
discovering dark ecstasy.
Scattering silver, running, we
broke writhing through the black and white,
each ripple bearing a spear of light,

and swam with tongues of water in
our thighs, rolled weightless on the thin
film, sank like turning, weightless things
to the still weed world, rose, heads in rings,
and the way that flesh, slippery with life

felt, she might not have been my wife--
but was, that wet one, shivering, laughing,
tender in moon-stare, dream distaffing
rightly that time had come. She led
me, lie-drunk, back to fact and bed.

THINGS WROTE WITH LABOUR

Estrangement of the craftsman and consumer
appears whenever poet and reader wed,
makes each see oddness, each remember rumor,
and drives both parties aching from the bed
to live apart and nourish lonely humor,
one wanting song, one wanting to be fed:

"Come drink my stink!"
                            "No, I seek a perfumer!"
"Come anguish with me!"
                            "No, come ease my head!"

Although for lancet love he throbs like a tumor,
the reader will never submit. Ben Jonson said,
Things wrote with labour deserve to be so read.

SEALS . . .

. . . fluff white in the sun on barnacled ledges
as our boat draws near:
so many bags of flour dropped
with their corners in the air.

They flip themselves like legless pigs
or middleaged ladies at play.
Gracelessly giving a grunt, they dump
themselves into the bay

only to rise by the side of the boat
and individually peer,
each bald as a pickle, staring us down
like the wife of a financeer.

IMITATION OF NATURE

This soap ad shows, for no clear reason, birds
with geometric beaks and glad round eyes
sitting in nests floating in scalloped skies,
singing what seem to be mostly fifths and thirds
(as indicated by the arching staves
that imprint music on the air).
                    So bright
the tree, the birds, the blowing sheets so white,
so slick the page, so true the pledge that saves
scrubbing and money for all who buy the box
containing sunshine, that one trusts to art:

he knows life is illusion, that the part
of him concerned with toil and dirty socks
and ragged boughs and nests without a song
and warm, small, frightened hearts
                          is simply wrong.

FLIRT

At dawn a nosey doe looked in
our window like she never meant
to pry. She quivered for a scent,

her lashes waxy with mascara,
silk ears swept up, a painted face
on a lightbulb head balanced in place

on an ungainly neck and narrow,
shivering shoulders. She, combining
the virtues of the hoyden, horse, and sparrow,

appeared to be insulted when
we spied her, bolted feminine,
thick-thighed and little-footed--ten

rocking broad-bottomed hops and stopped
to see if we were watching for sure,
then--away! with a white jogging tail for a lure.

NEGATIVE

I have lost the print, but in this negative
you can see her shape, if not much more.   That black
is beach.   Her hair, here white, was black.   That white
is water, laced with black.   Its roar and that
of the wind (not pictured here, except as her hair
flies out from her grey shoulders--they were brown)
drowned all our conversation.   We lost track
that sun-bleached day (the sun here makes her frown)
of hours, words, kisses, sandwiches and beer,
all used in colorful affirmative.

We left our imprint on the sand.   The sea
or wind in another season cleaned this away,
and now all black and white in each our minds
remains some blurry dent of how we lay,
some negative of warmth of other lips,
some scrape of sandy thighs, some taste of salt.
I forget now how it was, but how it ends
is negative, the afterglow of a glimpse,
turned inside out, unfleshed, with strength for fault,
remembered in the nerves transparently.

JANET

1

Green, though I was what they called a Veteran,
and home a week, I found I had become
transformed from something of a scrawny boy
to something of a flag and fife and drum.
But Janet had an instinct for symbols. She

knew Mother, Nation, Church, would find me fit
and sinless. Meanwhile, I would serve. She was
lascivious as a banana-split,
this camellia cloud who at eighteen condensed
(vapor of Texas oil). A cumulous thickness

of limb and lip and tongue were her decoy
for a hairspring heart of deadly summer quickness.
A beauty! As one says of a horse that seems
impossibly nimble and sleek. And my embrace
scarcely contained her shoulders. My neck was stiff

from too much reaching for her cloudy face.
Too bad to kid the kid, after such sadness
and drizzly Corpus winter nights, the hours
lighted by yellow radio dial, coffee
in drive-ins, smoking, talking, parking--hours

in which, as for a child, she peeled life down
to its core of sudden horror: Nothing had
prepared me for sordidness, not Hitler,
nor any more intimate ways of knowing bad.
Nursery cruelty, adolescent animality,

gave no such vision of deliberate meaninglessness.
I think, to have survived, I must have found

some meaning life cannot make me confess.
That she survived, and how, is all the horror,
the rain of grief, the unfathomable source.

2

It went like this: Her father lent his car;
and nightly we would scour the spitting course
of wet and flat roads round the glistening city.
Always she came as fresh as advertised,
and always, before the night was gone, her tears

and loving left her pulpy, realized,
as a product bought and used. Harmless necking,
true, as I worked slowly--thinking of the sweet
family-type and round-eyed girl in socks
I knew before the spoil of war. To meet

a Postoffice mind on its own terms was my
strategy. I had read the way to change
a libido was by talk. The first week I
elaborated on the passing strange
and wondrous pitiful. Then she began

her tale, which was somewhat to disarrange
my Boy Scout Manual seduction. I slept
in the guestroom of her home, which went its juice-
and-coffee, vacuum-and-Godfrey way as though
the sun in a kitchen window made a truce

between God and Texas: There was nothing
to forgive. But Janet tiptoed in at ten
and kissed me under a canopy of hair,
and we were back in sunless lives again,
among the shapeless ogres of the heart.

3

Her parents sent her innocently, just
sixteen, away to a state-supported prep
school in a flatland town, Concourse, her bust
already having burst like dough, with large
allowance and wardrobe: College Girl, they thought

her, but amusing, as little girls who scuff
around the house in grown-up shoes. She sought
a Concourse Corydon and found one with
a car. Oh, *tempora* and *mores* there
conjoined. The pimply squeak for whom a flower

was something to dig pollen from, this Ben,
gave her a towel to sit on so as not
to stain his car seat, said in his insect way
she should stop whimpering. Done. Nothing more
to *that* than an incision, nothing gay

or very passionate, and Janet stared
at the whirling roadside raked by white sealed beams.
In her lap lay all the seeds of consequence,
the pencil point of pain, and high, like dreams,
throbbed phosphorescent stars: no heat, no hurt.

This thing went on. What reason *not* to could
she give to Ben, who went at reasons like
a rat? Thunder of tailpipes nightly would
echo outside the dorm, and she would go--
on a library pass. The Ford would hurtle down

the road like rocks in a chute. What *reason* was
there not to? Janet asked me, and my frown,
like a pupil's figuring a sum, was always
silent, as I still hoped to follow Ben
before she thought of reasons. Sighing, she

went on. A month took pain away, and when
she heard that explosive summons, nerves would race
beneath her skirt, and pleasure was but one
of her pleasures. Sitting in Algebra, she said,
she had something to think about. An endless stun

settled like honey in her head, a vague
superiority to all the girls,
to all the teachers, too, to all flatchested
people in the world. Her neck was touched by curls
like fingers, her thighs bellied one another,

and the mirror of her senses thus supplied
all questions and all answers. Even Ben,
the secret piston creature, seemed outside
her orbit of sensation. But he must
have intervened, for at the end of the term

disaster came like grades. There were sure signs
that something grew within her like a worm.
Well, then, confusion--how she wired home she
would have a holiday in Beaumont, how
she drew her money, extorted more from Ben,

went to a friend who had a friend, and, now
losing and gaining weight to contending forces,
she found a fellow who said he could do
it all by chemicals, and went to him--greasy,
thin, pale, no more than twenty--and she knew

this was not working, as he looked her over,
with his curling comma mouth, his smile of scum,
gave her some powder, water in a rusty
glass, said there was danger of a numb
feeling (she said she felt it)--then the dirty

pictures for stimulation (as he said),
and finally, of course, told her that they,
for medical reasons, would have to go to bed.
She did. At the moment this seemed logical,
and, too, she was afraid. His breath was brass.

4

At last, and soon enough, she found the mill,
run like a Heaven by Dr. Corliss Glass,
who, thirty years before, began a practice--
young, thorny, feminine, a budding rose--
but who, they say, out driving with her lover,

in a bad smash lost him and--joke--her nose.
What future was there for a female doctor
hideous to see? In bitterness she bought
an old stone mansion near the heart of Beaumont
with pillared porch two stories high. She fought

her fight out with the law, now offered clean
cheap service scraping women with her skill,
contempt and high morality. Janet, shrouded,
limp as a sheath, came to her, looked with ill
and liquid eyes at the hairy triangle hole

in her grim face, winced when told how murder
was worse than fornication, and the knife
came as a soothing cold caress. She heard her
child flushed away. Outside the city glared
like a griddle. Janet, by instruction, found

a chilly cavern where she saw life squared
in black-and-white. She left on dizzy knees,
returned on dizzy streets, as she was told,
for Dr. Glass made sure her patients left
her sound. The dormitory, which of old

was no less than a ballroom hung with velvet drapes,
now held some thirty beds, though that grey night
that Janet slept there only twelve scoured vessels
lay in the dark on white sheets starched and tight
under the tall open windows. Beaumont

breathed in its summer air, its honks, neon
reflections. Down the aisle of beds could just
be seen tomb-statue-resting forms, the wan
and passionless who bore what they could bear.
No sound until after midnight, when a groan

came lipless from the distance, a tentative
social tentacle. Another, a frog tone
testing the silence, answering secret roll,
and Janet, when her turn came mysteriously,
responded a clear sigh. Next cigarets

appeared like rubies in a line. A knee
moved, and an arm. A body turned, inert
forms were inhabited, the probing threads
of mutuality found root. Janet knew
with hollowness that soon these stony heads

would speak. Think of that slow black morning as
anonymous voices told, one after one,
defeats by circumstance. Experience
scabs strangely: One forgets how it was done,
but rubs it absently and picks away.

These spirits fresh from death could hardly piece
together what it was that brought them there
but felt some awe of fact and some release
in knowing, saying, every hard detail,
as though one might disown objective truth.

They knitted out the net of money, marriage,
until it held their flesh, their age, their youth,
in cords of intellect--conceived, but strong
and real, reaching into the far recesses
of the room, stretching out over the concrete city,

the fabric of sterility. One confesses
to the priest of his mind. As Janet heard her own
bodiless voice name nights without reserve
she was grateful and abject to recognize
her freedom from the needle-race of nerve.

The bleaching sun burned in at last: The past
was gone. She shopped a day before she grew
the grin that would get her through, and then went home,
the next year finished highschool patiently,
recovered safely. Her parents never knew.

                    5
She told the last of this when we were parked
three hours in a drive-in. She was holding
a paper cup of coffee--long since cold.
I had a napkin I was folding and unfolding.
It seemed a time to pay a bill. I honked,

we left, rode aimlessly. At last the slow
logic of silence gave her leave to say,
"You get to need and even want it so . . . . "
Depression trickled icy down my spine:
Was I to be the scalpel to her sore?

In short, she had so taken all my heart
that I no longer could have given more.
Was maturity, then, to be like this:
renunciation of what one has won
because the winning must be soiled with knowledge?

Hell! Oh, with what acidity is fun
soured in a boy's adventures! Janet eyed
me as a schemer eyes, as one committed
to the scheme. I kissed her brotherly. She sighed.
I heard that some years later she, admitted

to the Church, was innocently married, confined,
and now, no doubt (she must be twenty-eight),
accepts the sun through chintzy kitchen windows.
I am a fellow to whom girls relate
their old abortions, so have had to grow

the common callouses, and now no gory
discussion interferes with appetite,
but all dissolves in grey, like an old news story.
We all learn not to learn. Unfit to bear
the worm of knowing, we flush it out of sight.

THE EVIL MOUNTAIN
(after Robert Frost)

The evil mountain looked quite squat by day,
all open to the sun--just big, that's all,
and smackdab in the road. It would not fall
and was not likely to be talked away.
I asked a workman what a man should do
who has no heart for climbing, who can find
no way to get around, nor any kind
of wings--who can't return, who must get through.

He leaned upon his ugly-snouted drill
and cheerily said that I could wait--or lend
a hand. They had made quite a dent (the end
of granite, granted, being slow). The hill
(he called it) on blueprint was destroyed. I might
have stayed had it not loomed so black at night.

50

LUST AT MIDNIGHT
"We must love one another or die."

W. H. *Auden*

Nights are not silent these indifferent years
when both the brain and the loin are toiling late
into the blooms of wisdom, impotence,
security and such deaths. After three beers
the urinary tract burns morally,
and lamps beyond the winter window grate
the room with shadows, exhaling groans, clicks
of mouths, clock, springs, silence and grey tones.

The marriage bed has innersprung its jaws,
pt_alined me in comfort, law and child
(no mean rewards), and even indifference
marches the years with drab promise of thaws
to clean the cold grey gutters and replace
fire with sun. Thus mawed and reconciled,
rigid I lie, dislike to stretch an aching
leg, hold my breath to keep my wife from waking,

want no solicitude, no love, caress
or other sweet soft chain than sheets and springs.
(The tense leaves fly.) Oh this, my discipline,
or knight's ordeal, serves to supress
freedom for freedom, bladder for mind, refines
philandering. Unblooded fancy flings
law, wife, child, bed aside. The chattering leaves
fly lewdly to the sea for rides astride

wet monsters of the deep. These are no threat,
but oysters slimy in shells, or bats partaking
by day of cavernous hospitality
(bedded with glances, brushed under tables, met
on stairs, caught napping)--their reality
fills nights of friends, wives, bats and me with waking,
anxious with our hereditary trait:
The loves of man must wedge men separate.

I know no out: Love lowly breeds distrust,
contempt, deceit and jealousy. It seeps
by night in basements dripping toxic dankness.
Backs crawl with fear. Or in the soil it must
rot roots or else turn all green growth to rankness.
The bare bough sighs. Love blights the fruit it reaps,
ripens by souring, lights by burning, clasps
with spears--the gravity which keeps worlds turning.

The world is death. It is the stone inscribed,
crisscrossing wires, grey public statues posed
heroic in the park, the documents
that shroud the hallowed desks, the scarecrows tied
with cord and holding cups of tea. The scents
of death have dried, the mourners vanished. Closed
books stamped in gold, bound in morocco awe,
hold the obituary known as law.

A skull presides in all our pious hearts,
washed by each scarlet harvest, white bone giving
check to the stream. It contains the infinite,
parcels the flood; its socketed gaze imparts
propriety and chaperones the dark
of each man's closet, disapproves of living.
The coal white jaw defines all love a sin
except the love of the only god--within.

Yet I, stiff coward, will love until the churn
is empty and the dasher rattles dry
for fear of love's one grim alternative
that lone and fearful man is slow to learn
(the belly bloats with time's imperative):
It is no joke that we must love or die--
or boughs decay, the skin draws thin on heads,
and rivers drag their tails down rocky beds.

No chartered whore this means--decorous bonds
of caskets snowed in silk. My heart denies
that love and trade develop on restraint;
and Anthony's round arms, eternal bronze,
that held his Egypt while the world fell faint
(like Cleopatra) swelled with exercise.
Those arms stretched strong, embraced beguiling flesh,
and let the world (dry in its breastplate) waste.

When I am loved the world is fleshed with earth;
the scarecrows reach their corded, lumber arms;
the fitful phosphorescence of decay
glows warm in me because I sense some worth
even in my faint light and drying clay:
The snake is graceful to the piper's charms,
and stone and bone are looked upon as prize
in the certain vision of a miser's eyes.

And when I love--oh, when I love, delusion
spills like a golden salve across all anguish:
The rockets fling their petals with a splash
and sinking sigh. Thorns drip in blood's profusion,
beak-like and belly full. The tongue takes ash
for pastry, mud for cream. And nettles languish
in the sun to share a thigh with me. The sparrows,
a cappella, shower love songs from on high.

We cannot be unsubtle about lust
among the mirrors--love's most blunt expression.
No counterfeits--no sweetness, charity
or good advice--such wax fruit leaves a crust
on trusting tongues. There is no clarity
like lust: cruel, selfish, ill-advised confession
that the bright blade breathes and aches for slaughter,
singing its splendid arc, for time of sheaths.

Its starch yearns to be sugar. Crisp leaves folded
in the snow like lechers decompose, invade
the soil. Oh wife, spring pond, wake green--
nurtured by flesh born of your flesh, molded
of molds long dead, and here beside me, queen,
steaming in winter, love exhaling, laid
like the twine of roots upon my heart, oh reap
leaves, rot the skull, and then we both may sleep!

VALEDICTION: LEAD AND GOLD

Lead, I once read, when set on gold (for years,
as I have been with you), mingles its atoms,
fills the invisible spaces, making one
of two. Oh, we are melded! Parting tears,
but in my imponderable leadness, all unblended
except for a pressing surface, I am held
(with empty spaces) still apart from gold,
and you are held, and yet uncomprehended.

I ache because the gold that I have tasted
makes dullness hope for heaven of alloy:
so juxtaposed, I regret integrity.

Better to sever--that your worth not be wasted,
and that it not my own lead worth destroy.
Fusion confounds. Fission will tear--and free.

BALLAD OF THE JOURNEYMAN LOVER

A day is long enough to find
    a night to follow after,
a lady of the loving kind,
    a morning of low laughter.

He walks with angled elbows and
    his feet point widely wide, oh.
On either side he swings a hand
    and swings a heart inside, oh.

He waylays maidens in the lanes
    and wives when they are lonely,
and little girls with growing pains
    outgrow them with him only.

He bears a bundle and a stick,
    a change of socks, and sandals.
He travels light; he travels quick--
    and shows the world no handles.

"Just tell me when, my dear," he sings,
    "and I am yours for lending,
for whens descend on silent wings;
    there are no ifs to ending.

"The clouds move faster than the sun,
    and in a windy hour
the petals fly, the colors run,
    the sweetest milk will sour,

"No one will see me come again,
  and no one do I sigh for,
and no one knows where I have been
  or what I said goodbye for.

"I sprinkle salt upon the tails
  of birds I want to capture.
My melancholy never fails
  to bring the ladies rapture.

"Now in our grassy graveyard where
  we draw our breath and blow it,
our cheeks are warm, by dark are fair--
  but no one dead can know it.

"So lean upon the mound, my dear,
  and part your lips so quaintly,
and listen to the earth, my dear,
  which throbs not even faintly.

"And put your hand upon my chest
  and kiss me now, and wonder
if loving on the earth were best--
  or hugging nothing under.

"If you blush now, I cannot see--
  and if you blush tomorrow,
I will be gone, and you are free
  to say you blush for sorrow.

"A day is long enough to find
  a night to follow after,
a lady of the loving kind,
  a morning of low laughter."

CAGES

First I was burst. My rib
(or wife) next swelled with life
which split her. Thus a daughter
we contained safe in a crib.
The crib grew small: like a rick
of blankets, dolls, its slender
slats burgeoned, burst before

the girl was three--a quick
climber and kicker, she,
who rocked crib like a carton
and made us fear her falling;
of crib we set her free--
gave her a bed with bars
halfway. She could climb out

safely and in dark scout
for the door, come to the stairs,
where we had put a gate
to prevent her tumbling, half
sleeping, on down. The self
seems slow to save its pate.
Parents hypothesize

a girl's falls patiently.
Now she hates sleep, would
lie down never if her eyes
like cage doors never closed
her in, always at terminal
of tether like an animal.
Tonight, when I supposed

she slept, I heard a faint
scraping upstairs in the hall.
I went, and nearly fell
across her, trapped, and saintly stretched on the hard floor,
arms like parentheses
around her head, her nose

making a miniature snore.
I carried her, moist and warm,
to my idea of comfort,
kissed her, left her under
covers: asserted the norm.
Asserted my love, that just
and outer cage, which she

will come to, certainly,
as sleepless daughters must,
in rage. The young must wage
hate on all bars. All bars
must be shaken, must be dared.
Fathers must bear the rage.
And she, at dawn, like fate,

will toddle to our bed, plead
that Papa wake. Indeed,
no love is sweeter than this hate,
nor hate so hard as age:
Dear child with touching hands,
night, day, age, youth, our veins,
our very ribs are cage.

BY LIGHT OF DAY

Sallow the afternoon, and dry. Kiss you
I cannot, as on a gold, enlightened plain,
exposed, we rest like desert lizards lying
scaled, cold-blooded, breathing in the sun,
our eyes blank salt dots of caviar,

conserving their minute juice within.
It will be a long day, silent but
for nerves, extenuated, tough and thin
as wires strung limply in the wind, humming
over familiar electric messages.

It will be a short day, waiting thus
for what unfamiliar wind presages,
and each black underscore of shade beneath
each rock. Touch you, know you, I cannot, as
my scales are calcified, my tender parts

crusted, protected by habitual glaze.
Across the blank world, faithful elders say,
is travelling, black as ice, the night.
Wait, love. Love is now unfeasible
in this western light.

INFANT WITH SPOON

Having learned to sit like a balloon full of water,
you have not learned all, daughter.

Be educated by whatever comes
in the fish grip of your gums

and seal your meditations in this school
with a slow tear of drool

on the kitchen floor. Before you ask what for,
ask *what*. Explore

plastic without plasticity, pure blue
you cannot see into nor through,

a straightness stuck to roundness, smoothly sheer,
not lollipop, but hemisphere

alleged to hold *1 tbs.* (or three
times *1 tsp.*)

Texture today: You twist your fist, intent.
Tomorrow, mysteries of measurement.

SERENADE

Thinker beside me, as
late light, heat, buzz
infinite intersections
in an afternoon,
summer is ample. There
is too much summer. But
let the sun hiss down,

let shadows yearn
from roots of trees
to find Idea of Shade.
Then gnats (you and I),
fast loci in purple sky,
think circles round
and round plum evening.

And plum past ripening
browns, identity
dissolves in dark, seeds
stir deep in spines. Too
prodigal, summer,
warming us unsunned,
us blind as bumbling

insects drawn down
by wine scent, as all
thinkers sometimes fall.
Night is the core
of generality: I
am resigned to that
crepe catastrophe

which has me nearly
buried in your hair.
Although I fester
generous, on death
bed promising dawn,
a plum of plum will be
engendered there.

THE TIPPING

Slow building is best, the card-
on-trembling-card kind of slow
piling of sensation, hard
aching, reaching and just touch,
so that the lines of one skin know
those of the other, any thought
likely to pull all down, and much
turning of the mind, batting soft
as a moth with one wing warm, not
quite daring to cross the flame, intent
on sense and senselessness, the trough
feeding drop-by-drop into the pail,
imperceptibly filling, bent
on the process, not the filling, clean
and convex surface swelling until
at some instant almost unforeseen
you tip and sigh to feel the spill.

CULTURAL RELATIVITY

This, as you say, alimentary canal
wired for sound, which, besides, is my youngest daughter,
has her own outlook: noise, a hovering smile,
a verifiable nipple--and a few

feet beyond that a haze of blue. We must
not judge those with other ways of life. Sir,
although those random hands with flecks for nails
look quaint to you, they are not quaint to her.

Those eyes that roll eccentric like a pair
of uncoooperative forget-me-nots
discern a no more arbitrary world
than yours. That mushroom nose of hers is far

better for close work; useless, wrinkled tendril
legs are for snugger snuggling. What if she
cannot support her head? Can you yours? i.e., I mean
can you support the relatively small

center of *your* concern, now that your right
and wrong are somewhat more complex than milk
or absence of it? Or, now that the haze
is farther, is it clearer in your sight?

Agreed, this belly with appendages
will never do. We must exploit its fuss
and happiness. But if we westernize,
the convenience, remember, is to us.

PHILANDER'S RAINY AFTERNOON

i

Soon I shall see your saffron hair
toss as you glance each way in the street
a block away. I wait at the sill,
standing, pretending to read. Oh fair
demolishment, oh bomb-bright sweet--
you fix me in your count-down still.

ii

Pick by the puddles, light step, light!
Nor seem to see my slitted door
until you veer, steal swiftly in--
for treachery, such discipline.
The neighbor's open eye is sore
where you have minced upon its white.

iii

Door shut, inside, eyes flitting, you
assess this world you slipped into:
refrigerator's throaty noise,
a comb snarled dark with wifely hair,
a wad of diapers, clumps of toys,
and me--made flexible by wear.

iv

What have these days done? Oh, I see
where they have cut you--here, and here.
Quick razor touches, two or three--
but twinging, slow to heal, I fear.
In public, in the broad sun--crime!
Yet day by day you walk through time.

v

When eyes see only eyes afloat
on face (but billows roll, we know,
and glint of blue should not obscure
that waves have mysteries below),
when signals over seas assure,
we dip, embrace beneath your coat.

vi

Having come this far, come upstairs.
The bed's not made--but that we can
forgive. The room is littered: Man
and mate make sanctuaries do
service as habitation, too.
Untidy though the altar, come upstairs.

vii

I drink the salty dew of joy,
bite lobes of flesh, breathe fume of birth,
feel blood collecting to destroy
with scalding surges of desire
all elemental water, earth
and air, and, finally, fire.

viii

Skin plump with languor, all my strength
spent fitfully upon your length,
I lie like a tuna, beached, aware
of the clock draped with your underwear,
sun speckling the blinds. Hurry--
dear, disengage this hook of worry.

ix

As a rag wrung, wrinkled, mops,
then twisted dry may wipe again,
my ardor kitchen-cleans. Depart.
I keep of you some dampish drops,
blonde whisking down the block, but then
absorb my home with ragged heart.

PHILANDER'S DOMESTIC EVENING

No words. I swallow this, as you,
no doubt, are swallowing last words, too,
but, dear, had you not known, I might
have juggled a dozen loves, delight
for you in being grasped and flung,
for me a game of staying young
by keeping all those shapes in air,
and if none knew, why none would care.

Knowledge is evil. Now what I know
of how you twinge behind your show
of ease and how you bite to cling,
contemptuous of the bitten thing,
unwilling, though, to let it go . . .
How can we love, with what we know?
How painful to shred all and then
laboriously build deceits again.

LOVE, THE FIRST DECADE
(1948-1958)

Ten years ago our courtship had become
serious, as they say.   That holiday,
a New Year's Eve, when I proposed, was gay
as a Steig cartoon: a joke of love, ink-drawn,
moderne, all psychological.   We stole
upstairs in the frat house, there said those droll
and ceremonial words of tender troth,
then called your parents, who were shocked.   Oh, youth,

they cried: We had not had a period
of trial.   We said we'd tried.   In this we lied,
and spent the midnight wondering whether it
were more sophisticated to resist,
comply, or lie.   We lay all night, quite dressed,
before a mock-wood fire and made commitments, listened to Sibelius, were distressed
by Henry James.   Our hearts were full of wit.

Season of love!   Remember Christmas, when
your mother, free-expressing, danced to de Falla,
swung her behind too low across a candle
on the coffee-table, spilled her punch.   Oh, then
our wassail was mature, our gifts were graced
with dirty rhymes, deep feelings were expressed
in black and white abstractions on long cards.
Liberal '48!   Gone.   With regards.

The World has aged. Republicans have won.
Gramma can dance, still, but cares less for funny rhymes and gin. Grampa plays with babies,
rarely reciting Catullus, Rabelais,
or making drunken confetti of Aquinas.
We pop walnuts and grin all Christmas day.
The fire is bright behind our knobby stockings,
and the twinkling green is looped with ruddy strings

of cranberries. Romance, like a party, passed;
the hangover passed. This year sobriety
is heavy-bottomed as a bourgeois tree.
Back then a Wallacite told us in the night,
his finger wagging, and he too, being tight,
how liberals tend to fall away in the fight,
how stodginess conquers love. Love, love me fast
and witlessly: The serious years fall fast.

COLD BLOOD

Magic is skill. Plunge here in my bare chest
or anywhere. Although you puncture skin,
find gristle, ribs, your blade will never nick
my heart (which like an old frog knows the best
endurance, croaking lamentation or
laughter, remaining unobserved).
                                            Once
a nimbler dumb heart hopped in young response.
A touch could scratch it. Never saber more
shall find it out. My heart has learned to think,
and though I bristle with blades, the wise one squats
in a corner, pumping, not in terror, but
wary and knobby, its belly chilly pink,
its eyes like seeds, its great mouth gight and tragic.
All hear, none see or feel it. Skill is magic.

THE NOTHING GAME

When my eighteen-month-old daughter pinches
with elaborate pains a bit of air
and toddles to you with it, you
should know what steps to take from there:

Bite it or give it back--with sweeping
courtesy--look it over long,
or throw it high (in which case she
will fetch another). Wrong

responses on your part induce
a fit of weeping only relieved
by peeking around a handkerchief
or some such elementary use

of fantasy, or symbols, I
should say, the signs which stay, although
the things they stand for go away,
or never were--the names we know

to use in games, handfuls of air,
mind-forged and finger-felt, which have
some distant relevance to things
(things that are there when they are there).

Thus will it be: Into the maze
of the symbol-world she will waddle,
gaining some grace, with greater dignity
losing her touch with the thing-world, her days

all clock-begun and ended, sun
improved upon. Already she
is name-bound: Say *Bottle* and her mind
(not stomach) cries a want for one,

repeating the Word with extravagant care,
"Bah-*ume!* Bah-*ume!*" (An empty one
will do.) In time her life will be
like mine, exchanging bits of air.

CHILD'S GAME
(for J. Y., 1954-1957)

tick-a-lock rock-a-bye
chopper-chin peeper-eye
Janey with a crooked smile
switched her pony-tail and blew
all three candles peek-a-boo
toddled all her crooked mile
upsy-daisy ring-around
ashes ashes we all fall down
 night night sleep tight

we all fall down hold hands around
hands are home fingers steeple
open the door blackbirds soar
all the while a crooked file
of moon rain and memory Jane
hide-and-seek in hearts of people
see the pretty petals close
dreaming comes gaming goes
 night night sleep tight

SO SOON ALONE
(a dialogue)

1

With love I turn a collar.
With love I bone a fish.
With love I save a dollar.
Love is, to me, a wish
for comfort and enduring,
for holding, caring, curing.

2

I will not be looked after!
I suck my wound and spit.
I leave my love with laughter
and throw away the pit.
Love is, like spring, renewing,
for having, knowing, doing.

3

I know that you are bluffing,
that what you want of me
is turkey with bread stuffing,
not a lark upon a tree.
You bark and tug your chain,
but love the feel of strain.

4

Ah, you, too, live a lie:
You truckle like a dove
too slow, too fat to fly--
not simply out of love--
squat tamely. But your eyes
are on birds that dare the skies.

5

Then love me for my yearning!
Imagine that I stay
indifferently sojourning,
but mean to soar away.
So make our loving last
as though it were the last . . .

6

. . . as any love is, truly,
where flesh is sand and blown,
and evening comes so cooly,
we are so soon alone.
Ah, let us not be bruising,
but, dear flesh, using, using.

LOVE IS LIKE A WRENCHING

Love, my wife, is like a wrenching
of ribs, an accident in dreams.
I can remember only lying

in my lonely world hearing the calls
of birds with their ribs aching
with song, with love. I knew those calls,

but not their meaning. I thought they
were swirls of pleasure. Even the owls
croaked tragedy, I thought, in play.

And then this dream. I thrashed, my flesh
stinging from grass and sweat, and my
chest crushed as though someone would mash

me with the heel of the hand of the world.
Relief, then: Weight off with a rush,
and rising, inflated, stretched, whirled

into air too thin, dangerously lifting,
exploding, then, the scraps flung, rolled
and shaping to a mass down-drifting,

I settled wetly back to the grass,
hearing in sleep the birdsongs grieving,
heavy breaths splitting me as,

so ripped, I felt no way to live--
but, stretching from dreams a hand for solace,
I found you real beside me, Eve.

BESTIARY

Rebuked, I crab across the sand,
    all shell and legs and edges,
seeing no end of beach and sea,
    half-wishing there were ledges.

Yesterday I was cocky gay
    and spread silk struts of feathers,
crowing the sun inside my chest,
    heedless of other weathers.

Oh, blithe the butterfly until
    an urge makes him descend
to weave himself a second coat
    and once again transcend--

and sinks to blissful chrysalis,
    dreaming in monologue,
then cuts out into morning and
    grunts forth in form of hog.

THE YOUTHFUL LOOK

Chronic apologizer! Damn!
My moment of assertion is absurd.
Always I am slipping from silence like
a punctured, squawking bird.

Ingratiatingly self-effacing,
I see in the mirror no face, in the face no eyes,
and as I put myself down here
I disappear in lies.

Never to speak without smiling, no
protest intact, no searing of anger clean
or gesture sure. I walk in short
trousers; my knees can be seen.

I know my faults. I say it here.
No Hamlet, no, nor even Prufrock, I.
Accepting no yesterdays, I will say
"I'm sorry," and grin when I die.

The Dignity of Man, indeed!
I have no stature as I have no age,
and, if a man, consign all my
dignity to the page.

DIVER

A parable: You behold
toes tightened like cords
white on a burlapped board
and see below the chlorine
green dance electric with surface
swords and hear the hush
racketing in a tile tomb
overlit, too white, your thighs
too white, swollen above
your dripping knees (and each
drop hanging by a hair)
as on the balls of feet you rise,
your belly parting from trunks
where the hips hang, hands
lifting unbidden, and under
your arms the cold because
you tilt, drawing a knee
high, chin on chest,
waiting, ribs fanned,
until all stiffness suddenly
is sprung, the burlap lost,
a last touch of toes,
echo of lumber--late,
oh late is release of weight
in the spring, and now this moment
above the water, defining
everything: the right approach,
certain pace, life's
instant contortion, then
water and final grace.

AUBADE

That is dawn, that light in the west,
brighter than lead dropped scalding on the eye,
breaking the day of silence on the nest
untenanted--and strewn from the naked tree

or atomized. Across the new white land
no bough holds any dew, nor leaf, nor must
any angled arm of wood make shadow; wind
must not stir the unreflecting, hanging atom dust

in that white land of final dawn. If we,
my loving flesh, could but prolong our night!
But no cloud crosses the coming of the light;
no birdsong shrieks that instant breaking,

that day of terrible mind. In a granule, borne by
a wheel grunt? shield clank? clatter of chariot wheel?
on covert pistons slipping steady lechery?
Will silver hollow whistling sky fish carry it?

Or will some draftsman, coat on a nail,
switching his steel-beaked compass, setting a thumb-screw,
drain the last black drop? What bestial hand, like mine,
will turn the last dial to the point marked *TRUE*--

searing the skyline with a flameless fire,
powdering all the antique ways of blood,
cauterizing bed and loin and mire
and drying dark in dawn's pure, pure still flood?

THE JOHN AT THE DEPOT

Only at the insistence of
a baby daughter's needs
would I enter that shabby
genteel mausoleum, dank
with ancient airs, that oaken,
porcelain monument to fat
days when double-breasted
executives would pause
in a gilded year and with
ceremony before
the mantle-expanse of marble
undo whatever hung

beneath their vested bellies,
gaze at the tiléd walls
and oh so casually
expel. They had affairs
requiring journeys, and
obsequy of the attendant
was their due. Now we have
trips, and the Servant
is the Master, surveying
his redolent domain,
darkly slumped upon a crate
in the corner, vaguely
indignant eyes yellowing

alert to extort the right
to minister a towel.
He watched my misery
in finding I had no token,
thus was damned to the dungeon
of the hapless Unclean, its varnished

walls scrawled with runes of all
perversities, its bowl
a jaundiced pool of rare
deposits, lid a sore
of wood, eternally
moist of its burdens. There

and whereupon my daughter
had now perched her quaint
and lily stem. The air
was chemical. The tiny
became the vulgar in
that room, reverberant
beyond all agency
of tile. The tissue crinkled
as I imposed the fierce
fastidiousness of one
age on another. She
justly complained, but then

delayed to work and work
again the silver handle
and frankly piped (as I
bit back my shame) her joy
at how the water tore
about in noisy vengeance,
until, still under the eyes
of yellow, I forced her out:
And she yearned back. The palace,
the crypts, the charmèd knight,
the magic hilt, the chalice,
she was pure to recognize.

SERVOMECHANISMS

AS WHEN
          tires pull on the pavement like
a dry palm rubbed on window glass, the whole
weight on the springs swings and it gives, just the turn
of your wrists at the wheel pulls after it everything,
then, when with tremor of pedal you startle the fact
(you butterfly, guiding a cannonball, all-wise and all-
powerful, hinting the brake now, holding the one
right speed and judging just how much push you
will need to take a coming hill) and you
bring all complexity to bear on holding
Nature in firm yet giving grip (unless
bothered, tired, or in a mood)
                              SO DOES
the spinning governor with two brass balls,
suspending weight on the thin edge of speed,
correcting steam, saddling expansion, resting
when deep heat rests, and aiming devices know
and telephone exchanges know their navels
and what is right, and what minute adjustments
keep it so.
          They have old Nature where her silken
hair is short. *You*, moody one, beware!

Bottling works shortly will shiver when beer is uncapped
in Moline, any highway disaster will jiggle a lever
affecting production at Ford, and mechanical mice
will invent their own traps, perhaps, to avoid being bored.

The sealed and silent factories, soft lit
by the low glow of circuitry will know
and what they know they can perform. Infinite

self-knowledge = maximum control. And where
filaments pulse, distinctions disappear,
and things and thoughts of things, all one, and seeds
and needs and gears and mica plates, or mass
and energy, virus and protein, all one.

And meanwhile you there at the wheel are clever
as you calculate a curve, make consummate
use of the chemicals at your command,
but now the time demands you find a way
to live with interlocking servos down
the line. Like any electric eye, flooded
with light, you can switch off, or else, renouncing
knowledge and power, mutate, become beautiful
and good until you die. Drop out. Retire,
like a sponge on a rock, and then when the ships shudder
shadowy overhead, lie still lie still, and let
the brass balls whirl, and never be distracted.

PERSPECTIVE

And now we know what Lilliput must have seemed, all thunder
in this engine in the air, and all silence down under.

The river is a taffy-pull, cut sharply by a dam;
the village, simplified and clear, is sly as an epigram.

Highways, surely, are acts of God, keeping cows away from corn,
and poultry dot the lot like rice around a farmer like a thorn.

So neat a world as that must mean something that we might hope
to find, were we a mile on up--and had a microscope.

GRENDEL

Older than English: how evil emerges
on a moor in the moonlight, emotionless, faceless,
stiff-kneed, arms rigid, and stalks through the fog field
until finally its fist falls, forcing the oaken door
of whatever Heorot harbors the gentlefolk.

In movies, a scientist, satanic, with a spark gap,
his power and intentions plainly dishonorable,
releases a monster with electronic instincts:
Hollywood's pronouncement on the nature of evil.
Whom shall we send for? How shall we meet it?

In dark times when warriors wassailed one another,
banged cups in the meadhall, then crumpled like heroes,
till Grendel (they called it) gobbled them, unwashed,
they stared in the daylight, dumbstruck, religious,
their hall all a shambles, their heads hurting,
and easily believed an evil wyrd
(generated in a fen not far from Heorot)
molested mankind. Such mornings we all have.

A blond boy, traveller, Beowulf, bear-boy,
sparing of word hoard, spunky at swimming,
arrived like justice (riding Old Paint),
had to be wakened to harry the hairy one,
grappled in darkness, grunted and clung
and unstrung the monster, as one masters a toy
by mangling the machinery. Men of the warrior-breed
approach the irrational rippling their muscles,
relying on wrestling to reckon with angels.

Grendel in our time goes by a new name:
Old Mushroom Head, the Mighty Bomb,
nightly distilled from seeping chemicals
in coils of our brain bed, composite monster
fashioned of guilt and our most fearful urges.
Blame it on physics: Feign that evil
is external, inhuman! We turn to our warriors,
hating all Science, harboring our mead dreams,
hating intelligence, terrorized by instinct.

Send me no bear-boys when the brute crashes oak doors.
Although he goes howling, holding the socket,
bleeding and armless, back to his mother,
Grendel defeats us who fail of reason.
As the movies will tell us, tatters of bullets
rip Grendel's chest as rain rips a snowbank,
yet he comes plodding, impassive, stiff-necked.
Feeling cannot save us: Sober must we meet him.

COMMON SENSE OF THE CROWS

Those fabled crows watched six
        men go behind
and five depart from one
        stark hunter's blind,
and then flew down from all
        the bordering trees

and so were blasted. Fact
        is what one sees,
but consequence is what
        one fails to see.
They studied character,
        not quantity.

SONNETS ON REASON

Sour Grapes
Suppose that like a rocket our desire
pursued its target electronically,
adjusting to each dodge. Ironically,
infallible desire is not desire.
We have a foolish pride in aiming higher
than any object that our sights can see.
We much prefer whatever cannot be:
To get is not the point, but to aspire.
Rockets are smarter. So was the practical fox
who weighed grapes in the balance, found them green.
Judas was not so wrong as out of season.
Things wanted can be had: There are no clocks
in Bedlam, raving of hours lost. Their clean
hands click their needs away with timely reason.

The Clock to the Hourglass
I am the eternal present. I am law.
Unnatural, I click consistency.
I go in circles, inspire obedience, awe.
I hear the Truth of wheels inside of me.
No weariness shall fray my metal strands,
nor shall my accurate springs of Time be sprung.
No sweat shall tarnish my immaculate hands.
I do no evil. I have no heart or tongue.

A soul of sand you have, that runs like blood,
streams downward without cadence, without sound.
Your final grain will fall without a thud.
Nature absorbs you. You are a moment's mound.
Time kills you. I kill Time.
                      (And yet of mud
is made the mind that made me, the hand that wound!)

Footnote on Heroism
Greatness requires a kind of ignorance.
If someone follows a line, he has been hooked.
No one would carry a flag or take a stance
of valor if he knew how silly he looked.
Heroes would not be heroes if they were me,
or if they were quite all there up in the attic.
Oh, let me never single-minded be!
Belief in anything is psychosomatic.
Ideals are dangerous. A man possessed
may look good in the history books, but would
you like to have him here (improperly dressed)
in your living room? He might, you know, draw blood.
(His if not yours.) Don't let belief get started.
Like me, be open-minded, empty-hearted.

And Faith Dissolves the Stone
Between the stones the river runs. It curls
around impediment and swirls downstream
whatever flakes or breaks. Adore it, girls!
Adore its fast fluidity. Esteem
its endlessness and how it fills all space
that is not filled by stone. Rest in its white,
its blue (promising all in a still place).
Or grow fanatic--let its flow excite
your inner thigh until your blood brings vision
to the inside of your eye. Welcome its noise
(in which the only silence is). Precision
melts in the water. (So do stones and boys.)
Believe! And if you slip, it will sustain you
an instant instant. (Then it will contain you.)

Fission of the Nucleus
They say the atom is a kind of fiction
   (good fiction, as we know, gives one a blast),
that science only knows the right direction
   and tells us nothing certainly at last,
that reason is equipped for self-correcting
   (it makes predictions, but no prophecy);
it is an instrument for close inspecting
   (although it has no visions, it can see).
Although it has no values, it can measure.
   Although it has no hopes, it can advance.
It can be used to calibrate a pleasure,
   but looks on happiness as a romance.
It can explain, create, control, and cure--
and blast. At last we will know truth for sure.

Oh, Let Me Fear!
You say I am not guilty, only sick?
That Mother did not love me as she ought?
Her mother was in bourgeois morals caught?
That somehow economics failed to click?
You say that social forces move by laws
that far outweigh my puny little choice?
You say my words are echoes of a voice
which has a cause which has another cause?
You say I need not fear, may be assured
that if I cooperate I can be civil?
That modern brains are washable? The devil
can be cast out, my deviation cured?
Oh, let me fear, be wrong, be guilty! Fill
my cup with hemlock--but give me back my will!

THE SOUND OF BURGLARS

There really are no burglars anywhere
(creaking the stair or inching the screen door).
That is no stealthy tread down there nor any
such nonsense. But I would not tell you this

if I perceived the slightest chance that I
would be believed. Some kinds of knowing come
as the wind comes, and, as the wind goes, go.
Nothing, for instance, such as there is down there

must be confronted. You sometimes must shout
out Stay! at a bellying curtain, hound the moon,
cower in cathedrals, hunted, and then shout
down clamoring cathedral echoes. Fear

is real. So is courage. Such wind-borne words
resemble the absence of cheese in the icebox. There
is no cheese. That is real, truer than the curtain,
door, or stair. That sound in the night is you.

ON LAYING BY THE LAMP

*"In the myths and fairy tales that we read as children we learned
a few of the simpler and more obvious truths of life, such as
that when a djinnee is found in a bottle, it had better be left
there."*

Norbert Wiener,

The Human Use of Human Beings

Alladin, clad in tweed and spectacles,
a classroom Christ, a gentle gardener
who tends the rows of heads and bends the glass
and grows his crystal plumbing, knows, alas,

what djinnees florence flasks contain, and wonders
whether it is best to throttle truth, to keep
the monster in the bottle. Or, indeed,
whether it could be done. The truth, a seed

with universal backing, might succeed,
swelling an obscene root, in bursting through,
perhaps in Russia. That would never do,
Alladin thinks, and yet sweet were the snows

of yesteryear (not radiant), ignorant
black and white, when college yells were all
the terrible fury campuses knew,
and laboratories, scratched with scrawl

of formulae, were edifices of
exactitude. That it should then befall
that magic find itself turned ethical!
That power frighten knowledge! That coeds

scream and join clubs, objecting to the djinnee!
That boys, no longer charmed by gadgets,
take up philosophy! Aladdin, fish
that he is, shudders, and will make no wish.

VIEW FROM THE GROUND

Earth at our backs, look up along
my arm, my finger, pointing to
the upmost branch of that high pine,
beyond, a gull, a jet, then blue.

My finger at an arm's length is
bound by my bone and muscle to me,
and to the earth, but as it leads
your eyes along, it casts you free

to those vague needles (also bound)
and to the bird (still bound, still near),
some miles to the jet outflying sound,
trailing ice-plumes in the atmosphere,

until our sight outflies the light
and nothing appears as depthless blue.
That way lies freedom: chill, still, vast.
I lie here earth-bound, linked to you.

VERA'S BLAZE

Aunt Vera had it: Oh, I was convinced
nothing would wear like gold, the way she blazed,
a wheel fluttering, strung with electric dance;
but she turned fifty--and was reappraised.
I know. I peeked in the bedroom, saw her peel:

her shinbones stood like poles above her dress,
and how I stared at my first sight of Woman--
bosoms like symbols of all fishiness
swinging upon her ribcage like the lanterns
forsaken on lattice after carnival,

and flesh, in fact, appeared to stream in tatters
of crepe, wind-whipped, and too entwined to fall,
gay oranges and purples, now rain-spotted.
Lime streaked the buttery pennants of her hair,
and chalky pink were now the cheeks that waited

like posters for another day of fair,
that would not come (she knew it), or that *would* come,
blaring and bannering, fun for young and old,
with desperate paint to banish any mood one
might have, reflecting how has peeled the gold.

NEIGHBORS

In Arlington neighbors know everything. Not
    a sign goes unnoticed: No gin
bottles stand in the garbage, nor socks
    for the wrong feet may hang on the line,

for they will protect you. They see that no lights
    are turned on when you are away,
that windows get closed when it storms, and that late
    guests get explained the next day,

and begin all remarks with, "We usually . . . , " because
    there are no first times in Arlington.
Every child by the time he is twelve memorizes
    the myths that his family has done,

which agree with impeccable certainty with
    the things that his family does.
They say that the sea and the Irish have bred
    all Bostonian weather and woes;

they see that all life is embalmed with a plaque,
    that April Nineteenth to the last
rabble route is reduced to a fact. Oh, they keep
    signs of liberty polished in brass

and the landscape correct as a frame to set history in,
    the past safely past. It is here
one finds the pot full and time barely simmering
    on a scarcely perceptible fire,

and all things are known. Revolutions are known
    as predictable, safe in a wheel,
and familiar details of a neighbor's home
    are one's stone in a pocket to feel.

SPECTACULAR

They had it on television with
guest stars and music for children how
        this Jack
traded his mother's sterile cow
for a handful of colored beans. She gave
        a smack
for him to grow on, began to rave.
But lo those beans took root and grew
        this stalk
up up, so everybody knew.
By means of that same growth, astound-
        ing Jack
entered the clouds, and there he found
gold and went in again and found
        a squawk-
ing hen that laid. At last he found
this harp that screamed for the big bum
        out back--
and then, oh wow, fee fie fo fum,
Jack beat it down to Mama. Splat
        and crack
went giant, stalk and clouds, and that
was all: just an old story they
        brought back.

MULTIPLE CHOICE

With a particular pencil, pick
truth, and do not erase unless
you carefully remove each trace
of smudge. Have one ear on the tick
of time, one eye alert for the mon-
itor, whose eye is blankly on

you like a dime in dough; have no
notes in your pantcuff, for you cannot con the IBM, which has
your number as it has the rest.
Best to resign yourself, your choice,
and either pass or fail this test.

Choose one (i.e., you are to guess
the chosen one) and mark (not what
you would prefer, but what you think
is right) the nearest more-or-less
to absolute: Which you is you?
(1) the dirty mouse with whiskers in

your heart; or (2) an echo of
a bell that rings beyond the blue;
or (3) a dollar's purchase of
odd chemicals; or (4) a pencil
in a particular hand; or (5)
(perversely) none of the above.

ELEGY FOR SENATOR JOE:
A MEMORY OF AN ILL WIND

Where, when it came, did that wind come from,
making the grass lean dry under shuddering trees
and a continent grab for its hat, deaf in the roar
                    and dumb?

How could there be so much air in the air,
shredding the clouds, diluting the season's sun,
its spank on the lake like the back of the season's hand
                    to scare?

What were the nerves of the wind that wound
our minds like tangles of hair in the wind, our knees
in the flapping of coats, our spines in the fear of the sound
                    of sound?

And where, when it went, and the ache of no
wind sat on the world in the still of a paralyzed dream,
had it been? From these drifts of dust, oh where did you go,
                    great Joe?

A PIDDLING HARVEST

I was an intellectual
on chilling winter days
and would not say things plainly if
I could find other ways,

but April seemed so innocent
my sap began to rise;
the sun was kind, and I began
to throw off my disguise.

I was quite nude by summer, baked
and sweated, fang and claw,
and other natural instincts were
exposed till they were raw.

Oh, raw and red as apples glowed
all acres of my skin,
till skin could hardly stand it, so
in fall I raked all in

and somewhat blushed that harvest proved
I scarcely filled the cart.
Now twilight comes so early that
I best return to art.

DEPARTURE

(for Basil Pillard, 1897-1956)

My errand was to drive him to the train.
He left (forgiving as the sun) the June
ignorant loves, extravagant green, and rode
human by human with me in the car.
Words, our intriguing spiders, we held fondly
in distrust. Facts spoke: The train was simply there,

seething like a planet stopped in space,
his seat reserved, his briefcase full of such
preoccupying things a soul might want
at night, or when eternal countryside
made looking outward dull. The acrid air
of the depot made us hope that progress might

not be to be regretted, and urgency honked
around us in the street. That street I had
to traffic in, but he would touch it crossing
as one steps lightly on a stone, mindful
only of what he takes to be a shore.
What words for now? Those creatures squatted dark

and anxious in webs back in our brains. We smiled
assurance that when we were whirled away
we would remain as real as now, although
worlds spun so fast (the universe expands),
and I was fortunate to feel at last
his eyes engage mine like extended hands.

All this was wordless: nor speak of the felt truth,
nor the blast of vacancy in the train's wake,
nor the departure of the iron mechanical
indifferently bearing its burden, groaning its orbit,
nor its exhaustive pulse or wail, but there
feel firm engagement of eyes--across the air.

LIMB BREAKING

Abstract, the tree picked clean by fall
organized sky. I sat in the sometime sun
when, crack, a whole network fell away.
It can come suddenly to anyone.

And with time-stopping grace of such
stiff, heavy things, the limb was year's debris.
Sky and I, to this absence of limb,
adjusted ourselves, blue, motionlessly.

Tree, too, seemed full of bare things as
it had a moment before. Not when summer
drenches with leaf weight, nor when snow
piles sodden spines on twigs does it occur,

but in that purest, driest time
of quiet: One sits in fleeting sun and bleeds
deeply until some necessary
unit of sap, beyond some point, recedes.

BORDER CROSSING

(for a student recovered from madness)

Sibyl, wait out the metronome.

At the vacant mirror, stare.
Listen, Sibyl, for stillness.

Steal under.
South.
Leave home.

They unpack your things at the border.
Travel light. Expect anything.
The border suspends all laws. Now is nothing
when you translate to there.

Many return world-wiser, holy,
tender to busy travelers of here.
Their eyes are objective as glass.
The present cannot betray them.
Their knowledge cannot be uttered or believed.

> *Ocean lies beneath the waves, and*
> *earth beneath its motion lies; dark*
> *silence under sound abides.*
>
> *Under color, white, eternal*
> *saline, iron, under time so*
> *fitful in exploding tides.*

THE BREAKING OF HOSS

(a fabliau of the Kiamichis)

The things that happen on a mountain
often are beyond all counting,
for when mankind goes back to nature,
those that flirt begin to lecher,
and those that lie begin to steal,
and those that flinch just take to heel.
The night that Bridgley found this out
there was a taste like sauerkraut
or vomit in his city gullet.
He thought--and he could not expel it--
that his *d'etre* had no *raison,*
so he made tracks for civilization.

He went into the Kiamichis
to get some rest and drink and fishes,
to observe the Oklahoma culture--
so free from painting, books, and sculpture--
to teach his city wife to rough it.
(As a boy he used to love it.)
After leases, deeds, and deals, his plan
was to become a total man,
or prove, at least, his animal worth
with his head in whiskey, feet on earth.

The locals were politely curious--
with their sure instinct for the spurious--
and looked upon genteel stagnation
with a good deal of toleration.
But when the town inhabitants
on Saturday evening had a dance,
they invited Bridgley and his spouse--
who found there troubles fit to douse.

Hoss Hawkett was there, a rodeo hero
with strength of ten and mind of zero.
His eyes flashed light contrariwise
as riffling streams reflect the skies.
Black, greasy curls fell off his crown.
His smile served both as snarl and frown.
His jeans were packed with masculinity,
parabola-shaped. A certain divinity
had this soiled satyr of the hills.
To a tune ground by Victrola mills
he danced with a barefoot adolescent
scrubbed to a pinkness iridescent.
Bra-less she filled her childish duds
like blossoms bursting April's buds.
Like a spring breeze, her gentle giggle,
shaking the bush, made blossoms jiggle.
No thought had compromised her innocence,
but instinct churned within her ever since
she learned to know the curds from whey
and why the butter, packed away,
was salted, yellowed, sold for cash.
She learned to bat a treacherous lash.
This was Maud Sludge, who, tired of plowing,
hoped for a boar--to take up sowing.
   The fiddle squawked its canned alarm,
and the crowd was hardly drunk or warm
when Bridgley saw the lovers leave
and up the mountains start to weave,
Maud, barefoot, unaware of harm,
letting Hoss haul her by the arm--
and Bridgley neither smiled nor shuddered,
not knowing which side had been buttered,
i.e., if domestic brutes were breeding
or human human was misleading,

or which was doing harm to which,
who tickled whom, who scratched whose itch.
    An hour Bridgley's wonder burned.
    (The rest were dancing unconcerned.)
And the dark mountain hung above
the lights too gay for mountain love,
and Ma and Pa forgot their daughter,
trusting she'd learned what they had taught her.
Maybe she had, our Bridgley thought,
and still he wondered who was caught.
    Then his worst fears took sudden shape:
Maud at the doorway bellowed, "Rape!"
and Bridgley led the dash outside
toward vengeance for this hymencide.
He ran through darkness threatening peril
till brought up by a rifle barrel.
The voice of Hoss showed no disgrace:
"Let's get your car and blow this place!
That brat will kick the slats clean out.
The damndest thing to fuss about . . . ,
but I can't argue with the thunder.
Let's go! I'm getting out from under!"
    With Bridgley driving, Hoss in back,
they fled the lantern-lighted shack,
for Bridgley did not want to trifle
with passion or with Hoss's rifle.
He swung two gravel curves, emerging
on Log Camp Road, at Hoss's urging,
then twisted up along the river,
bounced on the ruts, his back a-shiver,
driving too fast, bent over the wheel,
tongue dry, foot shaking, head in a reel.
The headlights pitched, gears groaned, and yet
Hoss kept on yelling, "Get on! Get!"

A swift thought flicked through Bridgley's mind:
There were no other lights behind.
   But then they reached a lonely draw.
"Stop here," said Hoss, his whisper raw
with, Bridgley noticed, fear. "I'm hiding
off in the woods till she stops riding
on her high horse. Make matters worse
to try to tell them . . . ."
                              "Did you force
her?" Bridgley asked, mouth set in store-
bought grin to get, he hoped, rapport.
Hoss paused and then the car door clutched,
saying, "That girl was never touched.
I swear she pitched before she twitched
her ears. All them kind wants is hitched--
before fourteen--and every wide-
mouthed gobbling fish is on her side.
They won't get me!" He waved his gun.
"I'll see who gets who on the run
if they so much as show their butts
up in these hills. You tell them what's
the score. And you keep going straight
on this road here to Creekville, eight
miles, and then circle back by Cove.
It'll take a while. I'll wait and stove
in any car that comes back down
this road. Now get." His smilelike frown
froze Bridgely's protests, who knew rapport
at this time was a risky sport.
   Bridgley advanced a full half mile,
then parked, lights off, to wait a while
and listen to the frogs and insects,
thinking of mountains, mores and sex.
He saw his belly in the moonlight,

thought of youth and age, a darn sight
shaken in faith. To hell with all of the
joys of comparative anthropology,
this fiddling with the primitive forces,
this hope of living like the horses
and such unsubtly integrated
beasts. When he thought of how he prated
to his wife of life so clean, unspoiled,
something within his belly coiled.
And now he faced the chilling thought
of racing down the mountain, caught
in fear of Hoss's bullets, but
more fearful of this vision: What
if posses form to scour the hills,
and Hoss, in panic, shoots and kills,
and an episode begun in wenching
expires in blood and hate and lynching!
  Our Bridgley ground his lower plate
and set his jaw to face his fate.
The starter sang, the car rolled out
and turned downhill its lighted snout,
then Bridgley, his insurance paid,
careened right past the manned blockade.
No shot. No yell. He drove like a knife
to stop the hordes after Hoss's life.
  He stopped beside the dance hall, hottish,
to find them dancing to a schottische.
Memory of that wild-eyed youth
upon the mountain seemed uncouth.
Maud's parents pranced in skirt and boots;
the recording called to deeper roots
than vengeance for a child's undoing.
And where was Maud, who should be mewing
after her innocence transgressed?

Bridgley inquired. Her father, pressed,
and flushed (from dancing) at last said
that Maud had been whipped and sent to bed.
Why that little bitch, our Bridgley thought,
fooled no one but me. She should be taught
that torturing Hoss is playing with fire.
Suppose he shot me for that liar!
And think of Hoss: He's frightened still
and huddling cold upon a hill
for nothing! Maud needs more than whipping,
thought Bridgley, toward her cabin tripping.
Maud's window stopped our Bridgley dead,
for Hoss was sitting on her bed,
and there before his startled sight
Maud turned the wick and doused the light.
He made it quickly, Bridgley mused,
but, then, that Hoss is surely used
to darkened mountain ways. Some wiser,
Bridgley found he could not despise her,
in fact respected Maud, but packed
that night and scrammed. The cards were stacked:
In conscience he could not have tarried
to see Maud swell and Hoss get married,
or hear the law of the mountains spoken:
A Hoss is useful when he's broken.

THE MUSE AND I
(1958)

She shuddered down her violet lids
suggesting that I write for kids
or syndicate a daily sonnet. Worse,
I might take up sex and write free verse
to make an undergraduate hit
with girls who, in the drugstore, sit
and blot enormous lips on tissues,
talk atheism and other issues,
and spend long afternoons debating
which Poet is most *fas*cinating.
My muse said if I learn the tricks
I might aspire to write for slicks
those quatrains which find their repose
in boxes in the midst of prose.

"In fact," she said, "without much trouble, you
might lecture for A.A.U.W.
on poetry of health and cheer,
recite, and sniff your boutonniere."

"Horrors," I cried. "I want to be
a *se*rious poet--who writes for free
(except for an occasional corker
fit for *Atlantic* or the *New Yorker*).
I am an *ar*tist with my eyes
on the N.B.A. and the Nobel Prize.
I want to be revered, not paid,
for sixty pages a decade.
I want to string a metric fence
around a pure experience
and catch the trauma of my times
in broken phrases, dissonant rhymes
and images that split the sun,

thoughts seen in a stereopticon,
appearing deeper than they are,
or kaleidoscopic as a star
with shifting bits of ambiguity,
intriguing for a perpetuity . . . "

"Can it," she said. "You think that you
can ever attain the cosmic view,
the voice with timbre, or procure
an academic sinecure?"

"I must," I said. "Consider: I'm
applying for a Guggenheim!"

"Well, if your collar is not dirty,
you're true to your wife and over thirty
(so won't be 'younger' many more years),
have hair cut well above your ears,
and students call you 'good old guy,'
I guess you roughly qualify.
Now, first, collect a coterie . . ."

"Wait! I want to write *poetry!*"

"Don't interrupt. I'm teaching you.
There are several things you have to do:
Make anti-scientific taunts,
and hail a West Coast Renaissance,
but court the *Kenyon-Swanee* axis
with poetry that bores, relaxes;
warble a colorless coloratura,
memorize every *Botteghe Oscure* . . . "

"I want to *write!* I've got the call!"

"Oh, son, write seldom, if at all.
But, if you must, all sense disjoint:
Poetry must not have a point.
And break the iamb, lose the beat;
a sense of rhythm means defeat.
Abuse the public's brain and ear,
and learn this motto: *Be not clear*.
Rare language is your diadem,
and words are blossoms: Rest on them
like a butterfly and aspirate,
for sentences are out of date.
Allude to languages that you
find quoted in some old review.
Your titles should be borrowed Latin,
the lines below like shreds of satin.
Let no one see how thoughts are linked:
magnificently indistinct!
Your touch with life you have to cure:
Draw all your stuff from literature.
Your showmanship is simply null:
Be precious, difficult, and dull.
And, last, I speak a word I hate:
Never," she gagged, "communicate!"

1 9 5 9 - 1 9 6 3

In 1959 I spent a couple of months at the Huntington Hartford
Foundation (at that time an artists' colony near Los Angeles).
There I did most of the final work on the verse plays which were
later to be collected as *Plays for an Imaginary Theater*, and I
wrote the series, "Instructions for Acting." The next year I
received the Amy Lowell Poetry Traveling Scholarship, with its
interesting requirement that the poet spend a year outside continental United States. We went to England, found a cottage in
Sussex, entered Michelle and Beth in a private school nearby,
and I worked by an electric fire all winter on novels. (*The Fell
of Dark* was later published; the other, *Theodore and the Mermaid*,
was not, except for one poem taken from it, "The Ocean's Warning
to the Skindiver,"--written in Sussex long before I was ever
skindiving.) In the spring of 1961 we rented an apartment in
Cadiz, where we lived for six months. I was writing fiction and
poetry, but mostly we wrestled with Spanish, drank cheap wine,
went to bull fights, and swam a lot. I had started my monthly
column on poetry for *Writer's Digest* in 1959, and the columns I
mailed back from Europe constitute the core of the technical
portions of *The Poet and the Poem*.

We returned reluctantly to Ohio. The editor of Golden Quill
Press requested a manuscript for the Book Club for Poetry, so I
skimmed my work to that time for *Light in the West*, which appeared
in 1962. Michelle had had a severe allergic condition from birth,
and it worsened when we returned from Europe. Advised to seek
another change in climate, we tagged along with our close friends
Frankie and Phil Ruopp and their four children to the Virgin
Islands, to help start a college there--on leave from Antioch.

These five years saw a lot more movement than progress in
our lives. I think the calendar was broken. Without realizing
it, I was already fed up with professional life, and the more
skillful I became at it, the more poetry itself seemed just
another professional activity--an attitude I fostered, then outgrew.

INSTRUCTIONS FOR ACTING

Improvisation
We have no prompter for this show. In fact,
I have never seen a script, although, of course,
all surely know the general story line.
It gripped us young, continues to intrigue
in spite of its familiarity.
A kind of dazzle from the klieg glare makes
us unaware, performing, of the fact

that no one sits out there in the dark house.
No intermission follows any act.
No gun fires blanks. We laugh at our own jokes.
Although not many of us have studied lines
and almost none is very strong or wise,
the show goes on. The curtain already has risen.
Fear silence. Look alert. And improvise.

Drunk Scene
No, don't act drunk. No drunk acts drunk except
when soberly he wants to hug the world
like sun-warmed laundry off the line and blindly
tumble--or else he's young and thinks it's smart.
We drinkers stand much straighter than we can.

A tinkle tells us when we tilt too far.
We talk like alum-eaters, listen like
lip-reading lovers, hiccup man to man.
Our insight blurs our gaiety. We think
our underwater vista, wobbly, blue,

is somehow truer than landscapes of air.
We reconfirm the facts with each new drink.
As children play at seriousness, we are

more sober, drunk, than we know how to be.
Our life is acting, speaking lines we learned

uncaring, but, the curtain up, we *care*.
Just play the scene as though you cared too much,
as though the wall might shift beneath your hand
(which walls, you know, may sometimes do). Just play
at holding something you can never touch.

The Actor Acts an Actor Acting an Actor
When you do Bottom doing the play, remember,
Pyramus, as he sees him, is not a man.
Bottom, you know, cannot act by the Method.
He makes his product like an artisan;
his Pyramus, self-conscious, struts by rote.
What truth there is in him is quite remote.

His Pyramus, in fact, is acting. Think
of that dream that wakes us all from time to time:
You are alone, lost, panicky in halls
of mirrors, crashing repeatedly into walls,
unable, any more, to know which you
is you. Your self recedes. You stand and blink.

Our roles are always taking on new roles
(as lies need lies to make their truths more true).
When Pyramus makes love to Thisbe, he
is more a wall than that he is talking through.
There is no final image in the mirrors:
you are Pyramus acting Bottom acting you.

Sally Gives In Gracefully
Now scratching at the window, Sally, comes
your demon lover. Gather at the throat
your sheer white flowing gown. Your fingers fanned

at your lips, your shimmering hair undone, you float
to the casement and unlatch the shutter. Drums
trip at your temples; burning eyes expand

as Henry nimbly vaults across the sill.
A glance around the room, and he pulls you to him,
your spine bending. Your hands, like captured birds,

struggle around the face which snaps its fill
from mouth, cheeks, neck and shoulders. Still no words
as he darkly drives you to the bed and down.

No cries for help, for, after all, you drew him,
as petals ask for digging of the bee.
Accept his scalding crush--though fearfully.

Curtain--as Henry flings aside your gown.
Relax--they have done it this way time out of mind:
same set, same costume, no props of any kind.

Fool and Clown
The fool now enters to the clown. This scene
suggests a kind of circling dance--a moon

around a dumpish earth, a terrier winding
his leash around a pole, tugging, binding--

a mind that buzzes like a gnat about
a head that sees the world without a doubt--

Iago, rendered by a zany, turning
a dark clown into a tower of slow burning--

the fancy taking to a curious fact--
or fine-finned fish that contemplates a hook--

a lady slicing cheese--a girl engaging
in fatal courtship with a lion aging--

a poet, licensed by a sullen world
to tease its snake of evil and be killed--

the swirl of water round a stone, eroding--
a stranger lusting at a rustic wedding.

The fool, of course, is free to flit around.
The clown must keep his socks upon the ground.

Sugar Daddy
No actor having worked as hard as you can take
the ample, easy view, the fat, hexameter gait,
without some strain. Suppose that you accepted whole
your secret, guilty ethics, that you really *knew*
the rich are happier than you, that, after all,
the world is what it seems, you get exactly what
you get, that bad nerves curse all men with waking dreams.
Shocking? Of course. We losers suppress with howls
the dirty sugar daddy retiring in our bowels.

But let him walk for once this stage. Come, squeeze
the narrow hips of Sally, here, and spill your mouth
upon her rigorous lips. She slaps you! Good! Now, grin,
for you know what she never will: A slap can please--
that half the fun is being hated, buying your
way in. You are not kissing her to gladden *her*.

No orchestra is worth your high fidelity
in this, your prosperous hour, this new world on your terms,

where guilt has gone the way of poverty and germs.
There is not day nor night enough for your pageant, crowned
with phallic fins and chrome, the works, and wired for sound,
four shots of gin for geniality. You saw
the way the world was going, padded fang and claw,
and won by simply spending, losing track of the score.
You bought out life, gilt-edged, and now would buy more, more!

So act that part--which means, accept the given world
with no remorseful nonsense about what might have been.
The ruddy lights will cover your blush. Go in as though
you owned the place.
                    And, Sally, pretend that you don't know.

Three Acts

When Spring creaks on with birds delighting sheer
from every pale green freckled limb, we see
the sun is made by yellow gels and hear
the backstage shifting of machinery.

Act II: an orange burn bends from the wings
and, like a Midas, ruins all with gold.
The heroine, once winsome, bronzly sings
to him, once shy, who shadows to take hold.

More wrenching, now, of flats. Upstage a scrim
suggests the hazy distance and the Fall.
A filtered spot, a crow on a ragged limb,
a mezzo wailing by a plaster wall.

Bit Parts

Pick up your tempo, courtiers, after the king
exits--like long-beaked birds you must have seen
feeding quickly in the sea's withdrawing, then
scurrying to dry sand when the wave rolls in.

The Tragic Situation
Forget about history. This hero knows
no limitations of mere time and place.
He has a problem--such as poets pose--
but has the means to meet it with good grace.
He is not maladjusted. You must play
at being better than you are, at standing,
clear at the core, upright in the sway
of pitching passion, play at quick commanding
all the resources of history. You are
all man imagines he can ever be.
The plot is thick--but you are wily, tough.
Some force which man imagines--some evil star--
slams, slams! Again and again you rise. But see--
the last act shows how man is not enough.

Classical Comedy: Harpagon
Through all the manner, music of the lines,
the foppish posing of the younger son,
deceit of servants, lechery of dames,
the silly sighing of the maiden won,
the treasure casket found, the missing father
appearing grandly in the nick of time,
and all the lovers pairing off and bowing
with a curving motion, final forcèd rhyme,
you must assert a pantomime of anguish:
The miser duped, stripped of his love and gold
(of all his crusty heart has learned to value),
tearing his wig, now--ugly, loud and old.
The applause is troubled! You have made them feel
that in this artifice one man was real.

Sally as Cleopatra
Your flail of exasperation is too real,
is too much you, too, well, revealing, as

one sees in a window, passing, some wife raising
domestic hell. We look away. We know
too well.
                    Acting is lying.   It does not do
to have your Regan, when Gloucester is gouged, gasp,
or Herod drool too naturalistically
as the veils fall.   Spare us, in art, from what
you happen, in fits of mood, to feel.   For you
are Cleopatra, now, not Sally.   At
the end of the act you die.   You do not go home.

But not that arching gesture, either, grieving
like an oak in a storm.   Remember: You are *Sally*.
You love because the book says love.   You wear
a crown because this is a play.
                                Acting
is honesty, the courage to accept
our false condition.   One sews the wound of self,
but self seeps through the stitches, as the dancer
ends on one weary leg that must, in art,
not tremble.   It trembles--like an arrow spent
in the target's eye.
                        Perform!   If hurt, achieve
silence, and do not giggle when you are gay.
Create the moment for which you must rise.
Now Antony has gone (offstage).   You are bereft,
would wail or drink except, alone, you know
the public sits, a spotlight blanks your eyes.
You keep the beat, and Sally blooms within
as phony Cleopatra lifts her chin.

Henry Is Awkward
Is that the best you can do?
To stand there limply?
To cross as though walking in soft sand?

To curl
like a snail back in?
To let the tallow hotly run down your spine?
Henry, you *love* this girl!

The occasion demands some surge,
some juice in the air.
Respond!
Greeting card sentiment won't serve
nor will the barefoot boy bit.
This is *it!*
No human moment requires such ringing nerve.

The hero of the play must rise to art,
his body must do
what his mind conceives--
and you . . .
you stutter, a passive fool!
Oh, Henry, Henry!
Perhaps that *is* the best that you can do.

Katharsis
Lean actor in your last scene leaning
upon your sword in the battle's pause,
hearing offstage the shriek of women,
        you give us cause

to pity ourselves in bitter action,
to fear the forces versus right.
Innocence cries, though. Take the cue:
        stand your full height.

You cannot purge the booted legions,
nor the storm still, nor blight subdue,
but purge *us*, actor--ourselves in this
        case being you.

A Note on Delivery
That line is too good to be said so loud.
Throw it away--but mutter clearly.
Some girl will know what is meant sincerely
is tucked like a love-note under a stone
(to be read and re-read when she is alone).
Don't worry: There's one in every crowd.

Sally Practices Guile
None of us understands it fully, Sally.
Oh, we lie, of course--cheat, misrepresent--
to get ahead, protect ourselves, prevent

success of others--the anxious littleness of
our race. Forgetting, though, we are generous
by neglect. Self interest makes for a kind of love.

But like black water in starlight this girl
you are playing now appears to have no depth.
No motive stirs her currents; she waits like a pond.

Her treachery springs from some chill beyond,
seeps darkly into human action, sucks
silently; her surface does not whirl.

Convey this mostly with your eyes. Your words
are human words, your body goes through all
the motions of delight, surprise, concern.

Kiss him--and worry about your lipstick blotching.
How can he know? His mind has gone to bed--
and he trips into that still pool, watching, watching.

The Actor Confides
Let's try that speech downstage.
Break the illusion; face right to the crowd--
the picture speaks from the page . . .

for though in general we
depend on normal eagerness to hear
what is said privately

to someone else, to trust
the gossip heard on the party line,
at critical moments we must

shock them with revelation.
Why should an oracle deceive--or actor,
knowing their situation?

You say this is a show--
the words are memorized? Quite so. But this
is truth, for all they know.

Designer
Build yellow Egypt here, or make
a geometric Brooklyn, grey
against a violet cyc, or gild
the woodwork to reflect the flick

of candles, ghostly in sheeted Norway.
We need a heath near Dover where
the blind may see the blind, a cave
for conjuring, a mist-hung doorway,

a sweating castle hall, an echoing
room with a throne. Let moonlight fall

through French windows, or bars cross
high dungeon slits with dust rotating

in the sun's thin stream--some set implying
a roaring stager bulging down,
scarlet as evening, a dusky queen,
a hoarse, "Egypt, I am dying!"

Sally Rehearses in Jeans
This chalkline on the stage will do for now
to indicate your dressing table. Sit
on this Coca-Cola chair. You must allow
for the several petticoats you will be wearing
and for your hair--which will not then be tied
in a scarf. Those jeans, I see, are a tight fit--
but you must practice grace, must learn to ride
on the air of your lines like thistledown soaring,
escaping the fingers of your husband, who--
as he stands behind you, conversing to the mirror
(imagine it here), chasing your light retorts,
charmed by your vanity, but sensing terror
in fluff breeze-borne, in beauty on the loose--
will not be wearing, then, Bermuda shorts.

Let art assemble noise; let rhythm, style,
govern the limpness of your arching wrist,
the lilt of your laughing, tilt of your unfixed head.
Slur language putting lipstick on your smile,
and curve your fingers, touching up your hair.
If the style is true, costumes will not be missed
(nor actual Sally, in jeans, unseen, unheard)
as we watch the thistle float in the work-light glare.

Situation Comedy
It all takes place in the drawing room.
                    We see the maid, first, dusting.
Action begins: She answers a bell.
                    Madame, she says, is resting.
The neighbor boy says Uncle George
                    is back from Zanzibar.
Now, no one likes this big buffoon
                    but Sue, the teenage daughter,
who also loves her swimming teacher,
                    a bachelor who drinks,
but has nice legs and suffers from loneliness--
                    so Sue thinks.
Uncle George, who has learned magic tricks
                    from a witch doctor, then casts
a hex on the evening, so by the end
                    of the second act
the swimmer is flirting with Madame
                    and Sue is shocked and weeping,
the neighbor boy, in the garden,
                    is through bougainvillea leaping,
pursuing, he thinks, a burglar--
                    who is really Uncle George
sticking holes in a swimming doll
                    out back of the garage.
Next morning the maid finds a letter
                    dropped from the swimmer's pocket
proving he has a family
                    and a record in Pawtucket.
And Uncle George, in gratitude,
                    or something, marries the maid.
And the neighbor boy can't swim,
                    but teaches Sue tennis instead.
It happens in the present,

any afternoon in June.
It hasn't happened yet, of course.
The doorbell will ring soon.

A Touch of Madness

Invariably the writer sticks
  in someone a bit strange--
like this girl you play, her pallid face
  skillful in quick change.

Her lines, like silk shreds, shimmer but
  cannot be pieced together.
She builds the atmosphere: Her eyes
  project darkening weather.

She picks up what the others drop
  and lyrically expands it:
She filters light with images
  until no one understands it.

The mottled fool, the guilty queen
  distraught in her loose robes,
the village idiot, Cassandra
  (who futilely probes),

the aged voyager addled by
  solitude on the seas,
the dopey drummer, poetic drunk--
  she is akin to these.

Her room is in the attic. She
  finds lovers, overhears,
as, like the Wraith of Winter, she drifts
  soundlessly downstairs.

But love is not for her: She fits
nowhere in the plot.
The writer has to have a way
of working in some thought.

Villain
The first act we saw you circling,
employing artfully the wind,
alert and graceful as you held aloft
your great black body on the swelling draft.

Then, remember, you landed
in a stumbling run, wings shaken, folded.
We smiled uneasily with pity
as you flopped closer. We were not ready

for this hot waste, this last act.
We cannot, sun beating, stand erect.
(Such a red sagging face! long-throated cries!)
We cannot look into your bloody lidless eyes.

Word and Gesture
Actor, the author intended these
lines not for those who pay,
but most of all for you.
Translate words now
to the cheap seats, to that Chinese
who wonders what you do,
has no idea what you say--
but senses how.

Miscasting
I can't use you.
You are shorter than the girls.
Your jaw sags when you are waiting for a line.

Your hair hangs wrong. Your neck is like a stalk.
You walk with a shuffle, one leg longer than
the other, yet you are not pitiful
and clearly would be dull
as a comedian.

You have no grasp
of your feelings, awkward at
the crest of love, despair just leaves you blank,
your anger bores us with its droning measure,
your laughter leaves your throat without much pleasure.
An actor? What kind of plays have you been seeing?
Who pays good money just
to see a human being?

Projection
The problem is to make your lechery reach
from these boards here to the last row in the house,
to make your silent kissing scratch their spines
like worrying in the dark of a nervous mouse.

The lines are not enough: We've all heard words
and seen our feelings written in a book.
Nor can you get to them as you get to her:
They are too far to see your aching look.

They hear but indistinctly, and they see
but vaguely how your lips her lips are rending.
The stage is a cavern, lighted, and they sense
a distant, common scene of bodies bending.

Well, you must put it in their laps. No lust
is vulgar if one feels it close. Perhaps
you hand there, in her hair, should clench in pain.
It travels! The spine of the man in the last row snaps!

Nightcap
Peel off your beard, cream all the pancake off
before the mirror in your dressing room. The face
emerging slowly is more weary than
that of the king you played--who died. With half
your life gone, Henry, you are living
each evening one foreshortened life: Such pace
is murderous. That king, night after night,
drags down the sky upon his head. Your head
must throb as you lie dead beneath his crown.

I saw you back of the flats, waiting a cue.
A girl was taking stitches in your robe.
Your lips rehearsed your lines. Suddenly you
were on: The wasp buzzed nobly in the web,
but the web wound. Not once have you broken through.

How white you seem in the mirror now, a greasy towel
protecting your velvet doublet, your sleeves shoved back.
We wonder together how men bear up under
their artificial crowns, their final acts,
the poet's blast of thunder, life condensed
(which is hard enough to take, God knows, dispensed
a minute at a time). Oh, art is a way
of making a living--sacrifice of kings
to charm the corn. We get what we are giving--
a nightly murder, life day after day.
Illusion, actor, sweetens as it sours.
Let's have a drink. It was a hard two hours.

ADOLESCENCE

It seems someone injected, as you slept,
a drug that made you urgently inept.
You have no words for clouds that cloud your brain
and watch ideas gurgling down the drain
too soon to be identified. You swagger
like some Venetian wearing a new dagger--
yet always you are shadowed by a doubt
you will know when you ought to pull it out.
History you dismiss with smart contempt.
You started Time. You'll end it. You have dreamt
of Hell--and want it--but your crimes are folly.
You slip back into grace with melancholy.

They say that Alexander, once, like you,
jingled the world in his pocket, with nothing to do.

RECEPTIONIST

Girl, give me none of your secretary smile.
That sheer blouse shows your armor: I fear you,
wielding precisely with your finger file,

wearing a stabbing horn on either shoe.
We break upon your desk like waves, we men,
and seat ourselves, and none of us gets through.

Do porcupines make love? I ask you then.
You check the calendar-appointment book.
No time this afternoon. Will you come again?

I will not come again. Please, honey, *look*.
You spin upon your chair and check the file.
The phone rings, but you leave it on the hook,

you good girl, cool girl, who can sew and cook,
without reception, nor being taken in,
armed to the teeth for any rendezvous . . . .

That ringing, ringing! And you smile and smile.

ALCOHOLIC

My father (didn't everybody's?) drank--
the Dread Disease, plague of his generation--
and we were patient, swallowed down his spite,
and understood him as he thrashed and sank,
and all forgave (oh, life means brief duration!)
and all refrained from saying wrong or right.
We knew, in dry, bright Oklahoma City,
the only cure for drink was love and pity.
We knew the flesh was frail, with delicate breath,
and so indulged each other into death.

But when he dared me--cursing me, demanding--
and shuffling scrawnily down halls of my mind,
sagging his jaw, speaking with tongue gone blind,
should I have answered him with understanding?
He cannot help the things he does, we said.
(He grinned and snitched a ten and drove off, weaving.)
His heart, we said, is spotless--but his head
disturbed. (Late I would hear him: racketing, heaving.)

Years after he was gone I think I saw
how we insulted him, drove him along:
His spirit we called nerves, said nerves were raw,
denied his holy sanction to be wrong.
The sonofabitch (God bless him) drank and died
because we understood away his pride.

NOT EVEN A BRIDGE

Across the creek--you cannot see from here,
but where those oaks hump over huddling their
summertime mysteries--
                        a house, barn, sheds,
spread all in darkness, grassless in brown decay.

On this side trees never attain such size,
and we have roads and fields and sun.
                                    It may
have been disease. More likely hunger. I
forget what people used to say.
                            Once, as a
a boy, I came down off that mountain carrying
squirrels, alone, and stepped into their clearing
as into a cave. A chill was in the air.
A hen muttered and ran into the barn.
A loose gate ached to silence. Silence, save
for the growling of the creek, and darkness, save
for scattered coins of sun in the brown dry silence.
The house hunched still, the barnlot bare, but by
the well a man stood gaunt, arrested, his
dark hand on the white bare arm of his little girl,
both of them staring.
                    I, of course, said *Hi*.
From somewhere a hound gruffed greeting. When
I left, perhaps they moved. If they had been speaking,
perhaps they spoke again.
                        Oh, we fished up
and down, hunted the hills, and saw them seldom.
They never returned our wave. Such hate. Or fear.
Skittish as chipmunks, they would stand on the bank
and back into the brush if we drew near.

And then they were gone, their stock, their chickens, gone,
their buildings no more silent than before.
Kids played there some, but ghosts were in the air,
and snakes and spiders under boards.
                                    So queer,
that people tried to live so long and hard
with nothing but each other, no cultivation
that I ever saw, no crops, no trips to the store--
as though a family were a cage, or world . . .
Not even a bridge to get from there to here.

                        NO SUCH

            Poet, there is no such place
            as in an orange spot of sun
            a wooden tub (moss-slick, brimming)
            catches the drip of the pump--

            where the dog drinks, and the lizard
            (pulsing his head) drinks and waits
            and warms. Such pines never stand
            in such hills. And that girl rinsing

            her tin pitcher, flinging water
            like jewels into the sunny air
            or pumping with a round brown arm
            or leaning to drink, her hair

            falling, her blouse heavy, a blur
            of the image of treetops and girl
            when water drips into the still
            tub--wanderer, there is no such girl.

DESCENT OF MAN

After a month in the Rockies, Mike's arms hung,
his jaw hung, his beard was matted black around
a stagnant mouth. His eyes, lumpish in membranes,
hung in their pods as he sat by the fire.
Our burros, hobbled on the meadow, grazed like a pair

of Greeks relieved of animality--
but we had let centuries take us, sank
in the lunar ebb, the slime of the past. These blue
peaks had not brought the grandeur boys require
just at the age they sniff themselves in fear.

We had reverted: the fish we mostly fed
upon were fried, now, trailing intestines, pasted
with scales, and soon we would, with beak or paw,
lift them out wriggling, eat them raw. I broke.
A look at Mike at breakfast made me choke.

I shook my skinny arms and screamed (while silent
mountains averted their faces like polite
neighbors). I kicked my dew-damp bedroll. I
was going home. Home in my mind was sheets,
radio music, sanitary streets.

Bride-like, I had found exudation in
the exercise of life. I sought my dream,
where things were starched and done for one in kitchens.
Mike, huge in his blundering haste, packed up, agreed--
like one who had exposed what he should hide.

We rolled our stuff in tarps and scuffed the fire.
An hour later we were filing down
a cliff lip overlooking the glinting river,
Mike goading our two burros, their great packs
rocking our rhythm, winding past the rocks

with aspen epaulets--just like the books
said outdoors ought to be. Civility
regained, we watched the leaves--grace in their gold
going--and how the woods decayed with pride,
and nodding burros took *their* waste in stride.

A SENSE OF SIN

Under the house was inside of the world--
that tangle of pipe and wire where Nature worked
her juices of supply, evacuation--

the strands and arteries, the acrid groin.
Such play was serious: We wormed under,
earthbound. Above, the toilet flushed like thunder.

No dirt was dirtier: Nails, splinters, bottles
threatened, and spiders laced the ways of hell.
Ah, we were seekers. Sissies stayed behind,

never to breathe dark air, the chill within.
A sense of sin required us so to suffer
what sin itself impelled us to discover.

FLIGHT BY INSTRUMENTS

After, at Cincinnati, the March morning scabs of snow
along the runway, the roaring lift in a basement of atmosphere,
and, inside, signs (no smoking, fasten belts) blinked off,
after the pull off up in grey absorbing air,

we drowned in spit-thick fog, unstirred by our engines,
our thrashing doubtfulness, struggle from depth, beating
the neutral gas. We could not see from here to there,
but followed, we knew, up front, some gadget tweeting.

From the seat behind the wing, values, though, were gone:
no forward, backward, up nor down, nor color in the fog.
Even the engine thunder seemed subjective. A fear
that anything might materialize gave way to a negative nag

that there was nothing anywhere to hit. But when
one wing, like a swimmer's arm, broke through, and we heaved
our great silver weight into the clear, the pale Spring sun
grinned foolishly alone, a seal of foil, to be believed,

assertive on a blank blue document. That simple sun
was glad as reason as we sped on a straight course, now, high
above the clouds curled innocent as lard: Inside
we reached for magazines. Our engines hummed to the day,

until Dayton called us down, to sigh through all
that fog again, and East and South were only in the mind.
We turned our topcoats, spattered on the bottom of the tank,
snarled in traffic along thin highways of the land,

more faithful, though, for our one brief trip in the sun,
which must be, still, silly as a saint, up there
above this spew we breathe--not to God, but to sun and color,
to up and down, to men who ride the ether like a prayer.

RECONSTRUCTION OF PEOPLE

In those days occurred mornings when sun arrived on earth
in yellow pools on green grass. Trees made shade.
People had glass windows, watched birds hop for insects,
or read news over juice, coffee, eggs, toast, marmalade.

Later it would be hotter, but there were inexpensive machines
for cooling and cleaning the air, others for cooling beer,
others for bringing communication into the home or shelter:
music, comedians, baseball, warnings, and, once, all clear.

And all *was* clear--of vegetation, birds, bugs, cities.
The sky was clear of stars, the year of seasons and days.
My sockets smart. My respiration is not free
as I think of our level land, drink the foul haze,

and reconstruct those mornings, things, and people, people!
God knows how many of those there used to be.

TO WHOM IT MAY CONCERN

(on sacrificing one's daughter to a man's world)

The bearer, born to bear, desires, nay, craves
a situation living-in, without pay,
but with clothes, security, amusement, tenderness,
some nights off per month--and an occasional day,
children, neighbors, appliances,
sympathy, cigarets, flexible hours,
and for various anniversaries
a little something (usually flowers),
for which she will perform such duties as
remind you at intervals of what you lack,
scrub, sew, cook, wash, iron, water plants,
and squeeze the pimples on your back,
adorn the evening with her loveliness,
write relatives, make small talk with friends,
take care of heirs, feed pets, clean shoes,
and see that all meets--except ends.

As her father I can testify
to her competence less certainly than to her face
which breaks the heart with innocence and beauty.
I have taught her to know her place:
on the left, to the wall, ahead, at home, under,
to pose while one adores,
then hop down off the pedestal and hike
up her skirt to get to her chores,
to be modest in the face of worship,
shameless in service, all wisdom in her breast,
without other ambition than coming to breakfast
combed, made-up, freshly dressed;
and as to education and experience I swear
that to my knowledge she has not had them,
and for this, chiefly, she deserves
consideration, dear Sir, or Madam.

THE ALCHEMIST

Your touch would Midas Midas. A daffodil
instantaneously in your palm is golder
trumpeting than bloom has been, or will.

Your fingers release perfection. Older
are antiques handled thus, newer new shoots,
shier the shy at your touch, and the bold bolder.

Higher the tree struts, curling its roots
like toes and digging. You, the cause,
leaning and loving there, stir attributes

of bark that stiffens stiffer, quicker draws
sappier sap up from the soul of soil.
The me of me wakes up and gladly gnaws

when I am brushed by but your eyes. I coil,
grow serpentine, when just your fingertips
trace the cheek of my cheek. My petals toil

to be touched. Change me, oh palm that casually slips
into my handy hand. Oh gold and shrill
be the trumpeting of silence. Touch my lips.

CRABS

If you were to leave a burlap bag,
bunching and clicking, full of live crabs,
on the beach, tied at the top, stuffed
with shifting shells inside its sag,
each sticky stalk-eye blind and tender,

claws pinching claws--or nothing--clacking,
hard, hollow bodies scraping as
legs worked them through the bodies, backing,
you would know how full of things I lie,
dry, out of reach of the folding sea,

inert and shapeless, were it not
for rattling crabs inside of me
that hear, perhaps, the long waves crushing,
the flute of wind through grass and sand,
remember the water, the cool salt hushing,

struggle to slit the burlap and
scatter in sideways, backwards courses,
like beetles, devils, flat as clocks--
these snapping wants, these shelled remorses--
to drag themselves beneath the rocks.

THE OCEAN'S WARNING TO THE SKIN DIVER

Bored, darling, with my public play of green?
You say you have seen that belly dance before?
Tired of my puffs and spangles, liquid shoulder
bare in the moonlight? You ask if there is more?
Oh, I have seen you drink away the hours

watching my grinding can-can down the bar.
I know the signs: You are rich and over thirty.
Liquor has lost its kicks, like your fast car,
like life in air, like habitats of mammals
(those fat expatriates, their blood salt sea)

and now you fit your feet to primal flippers
and, trailing bubbles, gravitate to me.
Yes, I have thrills of silence and of shadows,
a million eyes and whips for appetite,
all tentacles and lips and blue recesses,

until, entranced, you drift beneath the light
into the oldest water and the darkest,
where thumps the music of a whirligig.
Swimmer, do not pursue my coldblood heartbeat.
You slip from fun to love, whose crush is big.

SONG: DAYS AND NIGHTS

Strong by day,
we have reserve,
smile objectively
and love
passionately
though we smoke
Needing nights
separate cigarets
we turn our love
and joke,
intimately
go our social
as a curve
sunny ways,
seen from one side
live
is convex
impenetrable days,
but the other caves,
and find delight
so sex
in flicks of sight.
melts you,
kills my husband spark,
folds us to us
in the dark
and satisfies
our tight-shut eyes.

THE DAY THE CALENDAR BROKE

. . . was probably caused by Billy. Most things were,
like pouring syrup on the kitten's fur
to make her sweeter: That was Billy's job.
He was the one who lost the TV knob
so he could stay up to see one more show,
and fooled three baby-sitters in a row
by pulling out the cord of the bedroom clock,
and, all alone in the bathroom, flicked the lock,
so that Papa had to get him with a ladder.

Billy was good for one thing: being badder
than Anabel, who knew full well that she
was much more ladylike than Bill (just three).
Anabel always knew the time, the date,
and all the TV programs. She was eight.
She could read, do numbers, name her rocks and birds,
and say long sentences with enormous words,
could ride a two-wheeled bike, and skate, and knit,
and cook (the things that Mother would permit).
She looked after Billy (when Billy, that is, would let her).
She discussed the things with Mother that upset her . . .
and knew it wasn't a ghost, or giant, or witch,
but probably Billy who had pulled some switch
that caused the days to stop. (This--strangely--occurred
on Billy's birthday, February third.)

Anabel knew, of course, when, just awake,
she smelled the baking of a birthday cake.
But that was *yes*terday! It wasn't fair . . . .
Mother said, "Don't be selfish. Comb your hair."
But *yes*terday was Friday, and as a rule . . . .
"Don't whine, dear. Hurry. You'll be late for school."

Well, Anabel liked school, but Saturdays . . . .
"Stubborn! said Mama. Papa said, "Just a phase,"
and read the paper, watched the coffee perk,
then dressed to go--on the wrong day!--to work.
Adults get used to taking what life brings,
which makes them calm about outrageous things.

Anabel sighed as school was about to start.
As long as it was Friday, they'd have Art,
and that was good--but it was Clean-up Day,
and yesterday she put her things away.
And Henry was mean! Today he would be meaner!
And, she supposed, her desk would be still cleaner.
And would the Weekly News be just the same?
And would the boy at storytime still be lame?
And recess--Jane would insist again on tag!
Anabel felt her shoulders start to sag.
Days taken one by one are sort of nice--
but who would ever think you'd have one twice?

Just then a terrible thought struck Anabel:
suppose that it were Friday tomorrow as well!
Suppose the calendar were never unstuck!
Just Friday, Friday! Wow! Just Billy's luck!

Well, Billy's birthday party was a bore.
He got the presents that he got before.
But Billy didn't seem to notice. He
was rather forgetful--as boys are at three,
or, rather four. It was his fourth birthday.
Or, really, fifth: His fourth was yesterday.
Oh, dear! thought Anabel: within a week
he'll be eleven! Within a month--antique!

So old and bossy, yet so dumb and small--
and Anabel could never be nine at all!
From across the table she grabbed Bill's paper hat
and said, "You're getting much too old for *that*,"
and Billy cried and kicked and pinched her knee
exactly as he did when he was three.
When guests were leaving, though, she saw his sorrow.
"Don't worry," she said. "They'll all be back tomorrow."

   She curled in the window-seat and watched the snow--
white settling butterflies, so light, so slow--
and February third was pretty, she felt.
The ice on the skating pond would never melt.
Those glassy spears would hang there on the eaves,
and no more mowing grass or raking leaves.
The squirrel on the naked branch chatters and struts.
(She hoped he had a good supply of nuts!)
The starlings at the feeder quarrel for suet . . . .
How many Fridays would they have to do it?
Anabel drew a face on the foggy pane
and saw it all dissolve in tears. Her brain
all dribbled down. Considering everything,
she'd just as soon the calendar broke in spring.

   That night she dreamed a year or so of days
all just alike as buildings in a haze
(as from the Statue of Liberty she had seen
New York like fingers all with thumbs between . . .)
In her dream, each day the evening paper came
with news--and even funnies--just the same.
And every bath she washed the same old dirt.
She had dinners all the same, the same dessert.
She wore her light blue sweater and her navy jumper,

went off to school--with bumper glued to bumper
behind the identical car from yesterday,
identical traffic coming the other way.
Her teacher wore a very durable rose
and daily ran her very last pair of hose . . . .
The story--Suzy always got to pick!
The same old numbers in arithmetic . . . .
And home again. Spot gnawed the same old bone . . . .
Mama! she called. Mama *still* was on the phone!
And Papa, when he came, was tired as ever.
When would he fix her doll bed? Likely never--
unless these Fridays stopped! Oh, what's the use
of a train that rattles on without caboose?
Of clocks that go in circles? Of days that stutter?
Of Fridays smearing endlessly as butter?
Of living in a movie where the show
just ends to start again? When people know
what's going to happen next, they ought to leave!

Exactly! Anabel just gave a heave
(still in her dream) and without any fuss
found herself, with suitcase, on a bus.
She would run away, get off this beaten track!
The bus went round its route and brought her back.
She jumped, with suitcase, into the air--and found
that she could fly! The world, alas, was round.
After she sailed three days, or maybe four,
she landed with her suitcase at her door,
walked in in time to hear her mother say,
"Dear, feed the fish." But I fed them yesterday!
She learned to face the facts, and not be silly,
and wrapped a dozen birthday gifts for Billy.
In her room she decided not to pout,
and wriggled a tooth--which never would come out.

When morning came she looked outside. The day
was still its familiar February grey.
She sighed, but tried to hum a little song.
She had resolved to try to get along,
to take life with grain after grain of salt,
since it wasn't anyone's (unless it were Billy's) fault.

She set her chin with a determined air,
put on her jumper, brushed knots from her hair,
and went downstairs with little legs like lead.
What a disgusting family! All in bed!
They have to learn that one day's like another!
Very grown-up, she went to wake her mother,
who opened one eye just long enough to say,
"Oh, Anabel! No school on Saturday!"
But Mama, don't you know it's Friday still?
(Note: she refrained from blaming Brother Bill.)
She went to get the paper, just to prove
how stuck they were in this old Friday groove . . . .
But look! It's Saturday! February fourth!
(High of thirty. Snow. Wind from the north.)
She shouted in the bedroom that the days
would *change* again!
                    Papa groaned, "A phase."

(But Billy, in the basement, dark and dank,
showed Anabel a gadget marked KALINDURKRANK.)

REVIVAL

Sermons from Science! Reverend Moon, a man
from Moody Bible Institute, began
in Houston to convince us of his views:
The Bible, word by word, was scientific,
a world not good nor beautiful, but true,
the myth all tucked away, the soul aloof
from mysteries reduced to certain proof--
for agitated youth a soporific.

His stage was full of beakers, tubes and wires.
He could prove anything with a slide or movie.
He prayed demonstrably. His hymns were groovy.
He handled all the elemental fires
and in a week did most of Genesis.
He could extrapolate a wife for Cane,
explain what Noah didn't know (for he
founded the Flood on sound geology).
His sparks jumped gaps, chemicals made a hiss,
and time-lapse films showed vines grope toward the light.
His climax was to stand on a coil one night,
a million volts spurting from his finger tips.

My sins poured forth from adolescent lips.
I cried, I cried, for fear I would not be saved--
but nothing came inside except the fear.
Even my yearning for goodness was depraved.
I finally lied to be saved with the rest,
claiming I felt the spirit in my breast
and that I heard a Voice I could not hear.
I wrestled with the worm beneath my skin,
then, worm and all, I joined. They let me in.

I did not stay revived. The flesh is weak.
My Youth Group, so impassioned, throbbed out of church
in spiritual adventure. Mostly my search
was one of kissing every other cheek.
We listened to the sermons with our legs
crossed tight and sang our hymns like troubadors.
Oh, Halleluja! How emotion begs
for any outlet, turn it out-of-doors!

Science, meanwhile, bequeathed the true to faith
and took up beauty and goodness. So did I.
Our times are cool--and Reverend Moon may boil
with certainty and passion, like a wraith
with fiery fingers on his surging coil,
but he looks foolish. I can verify
neither my friendly worm nor my damnation.
Electrons are uncertain; so am I.
For any act, I know not any cure;
more facts, above all, make me more unsure.
And, though they would forgive me, I will not
permit my sins--my self--to be forgot.

LOVE'S PROGRESS

(after John Donne)

No temperate climate, Iowa nor Greece
nor fancied slopes of Arcady will do,
as the dark France of your eyes, closing, speaks
through opening lips in wordless strange Hindoo
to my palm isles and Florida. Travail
of love lures, in Sahara dunes, down under,
or humid Amazon, thrashing, or inhaling
the breath of breathless Andes, or, in Tundra
stillness, crossing the ice toward Northern Light.
There is no comfort for adventurers
beating across the iron lakes by night
(no purchase on the water) or on the shores
making machette progress: I am bent
for you, my India, my Orient.

LOVE'S GEOMETRY

Is this a circle I have drawn? I draw
(my perfect love, my circle, my soul's wife)
circles all afternoon: in each some flaw
touches the form with individual life.
These cheeks I draw to me minutely fail
to measure up to Essence of all Cheekness.
Being only me, not a definitive Male,
I love you for your sweet essential weakness.
Were you (my focus) any less defective--
tarnished, corrupt, warped, garbled, blurred and cracked--
I would not know to choose you. I, selective,
love only something less than the Abstract.
It is not Woman I would draw, but you,
though love lives in my mind--like circles true.

3 A.M. *(más o menos)* CADIZ

This hour began with a wispy *tin tin tin*--
the gilded chime of some parlor clock down the street.
Rancid morning of May. I went to look
(pajamas, bare chest and feet) from the balcony.
Dark scarf of sky stretched over our thin street,
tight silk shot through with stars. Cats crouched below.
One wore a bell that chinked each careful step
between the chimes, now, of another clock
in another flat--a tardy neighbor, with more
brass, twanging *tan tan tan*.
                              It woke no one:
the street was stacked with sleeping Spaniards,
oblivious to quibbling of their clocks,
to the motor of a crane down at the docks,
a scooter roaring past, a couple laughing,
and, blocks away, the closing of a door.

A mechanism in the *Catedral*
just then tripped off the truth: long hymnal prelude
of *campanas*, then, gravely, *bong . . . bong . . . bong.*
The hour *was* three. (I hope those lacquered clerks
of private time, those premature domestics,
tinny triflers, cogs too glibly sprung,
confessed their heresy in their dark rooms,
hearing that hollow iron.)
                          This *Catedral*
has a poor façade, but a fine dome--slick
yellow tile, a sun enmeshed, illuminating
the glittering, white-washed city all the day.
By day I never hear its bell. The whole
peninsula, jammed with buildings, rattles,
growls, chatters, bangs. One hears the shouting blind

selling their numbers, hears children play, or squall,
the clop of horses, harness jingling, rasp
of *motos*--Spain is a land of noise. Evening:
paseo, a roar of walking voices. Night:
some moments of hush--and then hands clapping, singing,
flamenco from a passing gang of boys.
The *Catedral* squats in authority,
massive beneath its yellow bulb, immobile
above the scrambling streets, white walls, parched Cádiz,
a dusty tongue in a blue and salty sea.
Bald yellow under brilliant sky it squats.
By night it rings the hours.
                              Listen! It woke
a cock. Another. More. *Ki ki ri ki!*
Impressionistic fowls when it comes to time.
I yawn. My feet are chilled. The show seems over.
It has been a night of baby after baby
wakening, of bites, of heat, of sand in bed.
Got up to chase mosquitoes on the walls.
A cigaret, a drink. I read a while,
a book about a poet who, it said,
"struggled with what it meant to be alive,"
in some particular century--ours, I think--
and then was interrupted by the time.

From here I cannot hear the sea, although
just down the street (in any direction) it rolls
its loose erosion of our rocky point.
I cannot hear the sleepers. Only bells.
The cat goes tinkling into shadows. Air,
rung out, sinks still--and time is measured.
                                          But
clang clang clang--an impertinent church somewhere
bangs its inferior alloy without
preamble. I need brandy. Three o'clock

may last all night. More cocks. Another scooter.
That chinking cat flits to another door.
Have hours no sanctity? Nor cats their silence?
Noise. Certitude. Breathe deep the oily air.
I love thee, Cádiz, for thy contradictions,
and write of thee till *más o menos* four.

NEW YORK

This is not a poem about New York, as the title implies,
or even a poem, as does the shape of the thing on the page,
or a personal statement (all my I's are lies)
but a kind of document (to be found in a bottle) of an age

of dinosaurs, as if dinosaurs had had some ferny Madison Avenue,
sluice of the swamp, of heavy splashing, reptile groans,
and some distant mammal caught in the natural network knew
eventually some creatures would dig up skyscrapers like bones

and put huge calcium structures in a cosmic museum
with Latin labels (ah, Rome!) affixed to nature's various mistakes,
and young users of reptile-flesh coal all went to see them,
though professors would prove that all the exhibits were fakes,

and this mammal (I) finished his bottle and stuffed in a song
saying
            it helps not to know
                        that you know not to what
                                    you belong.

ABOVE THE GARBAGE DUMP

A sick age--or a bad one? Look across
the weaving river and the valley there,
beyond that string of trees. See smoke? The air
is dingy: That's the garbage dump. They toss
the waste of the city there and burn it. Do
we say disease or evil clouds our view?

Or turn. Study my eyes, asking for you
(though law says Thou Shalt Not.) On this
dry grass, sun-warmed, on this lone hill, so open
under a kindly sky, what laws apply?
Say we are misbegot--but natural,
and needing, needing. Glandular be our kiss!

Oh, refuse of the city are we, you
and I, ourselves the very thing we hate:
the fouling of the air, the spoil of the valley.
We think of garbage burning as we dally.
Are we not judge and jury in our world,
our crest of country browned with autumn? Are
we not free, for God's sake? Surely we are right
in loving on the way to nothing like
mice drifting in a satellite. We bear
pain, brevity and fear on this warm hill.
May we not make the terms? No fun, so far
from the city? So bored, no thrills? So full, no spills?

Nature enshrouds us: Upon your lips a leaf,
your hair spread finely, now, you sleep in the sun.
One button of your blouse is still undone.
What sentry speaks as I would sink to slumber?
Am I the guy caught waking by the wall

to see life's Trojan horse unloading Greeks?
Let me pull the grass around me like a cover,
accept my sleep, a hero and a lover,
and shiver only once and then forget
that permanent stain of air across the river.

So, say the age is sick. Of mind, of heart.
The city voiding on the valley floor,
the fuming heap, the carcass half-consumed,
the crush of everything in the crush for more,
our rub of bodies, mind on other things,
our weapons futile, our defenses doomed,
art of the ugly, rhetoric of the lie,
goodness of a good laugh--or a good cry,
our inarticulate search for a hipster's kick--
the sick are innocent, the innocent sick.

Such talk! Poet, you are not doctor, no,
nor priest. The age is doing fine, your moral
trouble in time of plenty comes from trying
to keep down what you gobbled at the feast,
your vision of a world about to go,
from indignation: It is you who's dying.

I tell me. You, sweet sleeping anyone,
are, too. Dying and bad, subject to sour
delight, thrashing the snaky dream from your
forest of night. Evil is will: If like
that dump our age appears to us to be
so "lubrique and adult'rate," we are not mad
to climb this hill and (wrongly) disengage.
Guilt is our self, selflessness our death.
I lean on flesh and wake you with my breath.
Not need, when nature smolders, flames in me:
I am unnatural and evil, wrong and free.

UPON BELIEVING THAT SHE MEANT TO BE PARTICULAR
WHEREAS SHE MEANT ONLY TO BE GENERAL

Out in the kitchen she stopped my hand but held
the fingers with forgiving sympathy.
"Courage!" I said. "The others are all drinking.
What harm in loving if no one can see?"
"*I* see," she said. "Love is not worth the bother.
I am not one to drift into unease."
"Why, what the hell!" I said, and pulled away.
"We are not kids. Are you a bitch? A tease?"
"A *tease?*" she said, the injury reflected
in worried tenderness, lip pulled and bit.

"What else? You said we make ourselves unhappy
by fighting what we freely should admit."
"And *you* thought *I* meant *us?*" she said. "My dear . . ."
"Don't call me dear and spank my naughty hand!"
"Oh, men!" she said. "Why, only egotists
could think one thinks . . . could fail to understand . . . "
I poured until my icecube floated. "Men,"
I said, "think truth should be applied." But she
was leaving, huffy. "Just because a thing
is true," she said, "means *nothing* about *me!*"

SCATTERSHOT

Never believe them: Receive my words, my dear,
as the world seals up man's campsite scar, as air
accepts the air age, as time endures its clocks.

I speak as a pouting child throws aimless rocks,
as a dog snarls at a wheel. My bullets flare
from a soldier raking the jungle night--for fear.

UPON BEING DISMISSED FROM HER BEDROOM

AS cooler air moves over warm, the summer,
steaming in blue, grows gummier, though fair,
ignoring first high wisps of clouds--but haze
succeeds, the sun is dimmer though the air
is limp to the last, and like a warm pond, still--
until, in an afternoon, wind snaps our collars,
makes gooseflesh on our naked summer arms,
and all is still again, but thin dry air
refreshes us, the high sun thinly warms--

SO did my lower pressure give to high
and draw back south its humid, heavy heat
when, cleansing, cottony and tall, a northern
gust, like an hour's honor, rode with plumes
above my love and forced its low retreat.

URBAN HARVESTS

Wormy Apples
My motor mower growls grimly at the ground
and spits out apple shreds at ankle height.
Not having sprayed, we let them fall, half rot,
then chew them up with noisy, circular bite.

The air is winey and my trousers wet.
I love the chonking and the flying gore.
Not one for apple-picking, I am drunk
on cidering the earth with seed and core.

Black Walnuts
With her grey wind and neutral clouds
    Autumn is sure to win.
Why then this hail of walnuts just
    to do my spirits in?

Helmeted with just a wide straw hat
    and cringing in a hump,
I mow, snap husks that smear the grass,
    and shudder at the thump

of a thick-skinned, green and bitter bomb
    the fertile tree lets fall.
"You missed!" I grimace upwards, but
    morbidly, withal.

High Weeds
In shorts and slippers take
your chilly body into the sun,
all squeamish of the grass.

nor are you simple still.

Let me say, then, there were nights
I guarded the hall--of our own home. He claimed love. Love!
Think of it: finding him sprawled on the covers beside
you in your junior bed. God knows for what! And you
said, waking once, you liked to cuddle Uncle Ed!
Uncle indeed. I tell you I walked the hall, not knowing
into which bedroom he might head!

You wince, my darling.
Such foul imagining? Perhaps, but at your age
what can you guess of how men are, drunk, in the dark?
Nor was he so old--though he seemed old, bent to the stove
in his hut that night, suspenders crossed on his long johns,
his white hair hanging, long hands rattling the coffee pot.
He aged, but as crabapples do--green till they rot.
I stood inside the doorway holding you, seeing him stare
with eyes like little blisters at the cold flood tearing
the earth ten yards from his door.

Well, we couldn't stay there.
Help *us?* He was delirious--and nearly washed under!
I wrapped him, led him wailing into the rain, his bare
head tossing as he walked, white to the sky, until
he slipped and knelt in a puddle babbling of God--too weak
to rise.

So you walked, baby (thin legs splashing), scared,
watching me heave him along, watching us lurch and spill . . . .

You feed a stray cat. Must you keep on feeding? Lend
a hand. Are hands forever tied? In death not spared?
For though I saw him buried, I saw your tears . . . .

What sticks
when hearts rub hearts? What breaks between when one man leans
his shoulder to another in the blast? See--no
wind weaves in the corn shoots. See--the river today is still.
Don't stare at me: Consider what this springtime means.

I feared exposure might have made you sick. Once home,
I rubbed your tender limbs in your hot bath. Your mother
gave her imagination to the derelict
Angel I'd found--like one left wounded by a hunter--
working the spoon between his chattering teeth, and since
he had no bed she bundled him in ours. (We slept
on couches, felt purified by charity.) Next day,
rain gone, the sun broke yellow on his gentle head.
He took my fingers in his own and pressed them to
his lips (his chin unshaven), spoke with mellow accent
and watery eyes. He lay as soft as a pallid Prince
at levee--in my violet woolen robe.
                              Ah, you,
at three, were quick as she to mother. Often I saw
you wipe his lips where the egg ran. I saw your fingers
push back his satin hair. You never wiped *my* lips.
There was no need.
                      He lingered like a hurt that would
not heal--for seven years--eating our meals, making
an attic haven in our home. He taught you language,
taught you to call him Uncle . . . .
                              Yes, I grant he tried
to hold an honest job, to build a sober life--
but still he stayed, unfit as a prophet for the world.
Your mother took his side. At last, of course, she died.
I took the chance to move him out--respectfully--
on grounds of impropriety: a growing girl,
two men, you know. Like a guilty dog surprised, he fled,
taking a room downtown. He did not cease to haunt.

He loved me like a brother. Loved my wife, well, more
than as a friend. And you . . . . How did he love you, Linda?
Oh, Ed would love you any way you let him . . . .
                              I stood

restored today, sucked spring by the grave's side. You cried,
kneeling,
as the boxed prince sank. Linda, today the river is blue.
That hut of crates, tin signs, long since has washed
into the world's debris, that cowshed where we found
the weakling lover. Linda, he was old and smelled . . .
with his one stained tie, that barbarous hat (his ragged crown).
Martyr? He used pain. Martyrs have some use. He served
only as someone to give to, a sink for love. So storms
blow us to one another's arms, each Lear compelled
to bend to a fool, each fool to a Lear. Each body
warms a body, drains a body's heat. Linda, he is cold.

I cannot even lift you now. Stand close. This skirt--
tailored to shape what once I held in one hand! See--
you've grown beyond my grasp. Your head lay here. It hurt
to sniff that sweet hair pasted by the rain. Oh, Linda . . .
what did he say on your walks? Where did he take you when
all afternoon the two of you were gone--and came
in flushed to the table, eyes softer, deeper than flowers,
cheeks tight with private smiling?
                              No answer? And your glance
condemns--as if what *you* saw I could never see . . . .
What are you seeing, Linda? What do you see in me?

Has love made him invulnerable? His talk of love
for the weak, wrong, young, foolish, criminal, possessed--
for drunkards caught in huts at floodtime--these were his pleas,
reposed in my chair. He begged indulgence, really, for
himself. Is that what brought you to his narrow knees?
And I would carry brandy from the kitchen. I listened.
I was persuaded, too. Of this I stand confessed.
I thought I saw in him a Way, a force. I kept
his glass full, raged at my wife, lowered my voice to him . . . .
But let that force weave down a midnight hall! At night

there is excess of loving in the world!

For all
I gave, I was his last confider. Brother? Hurled
to the wall when he felt impelled! Oh, charity
was in his name, not more. Or say his loves conflicted . . .
still, think of the cost--to heart (dear Lord, to purse!) Though I
forgave and forgave again (your mother, in fact, insisted),
and daily I would go to work and leave him wiping
my household like a rag. I saw the cost of love:
Such giving makes us hate. What kept me patient? Was
I walking in his path, unjudging, suffering all?
No. Though I thought so, no. We nurse our own hearts first!
I bit back all protest, condemned myself, revered:
I handed him the evening paper time after time,
sensing he had a prior right to mine. Was he so blest?
To sit like a saint in the lamplight? Or, when he died,
to bring a hundred people to the door?

I had
no *need* of love: Is that why you mourned three nights straight,
indifferent if I came or went, the waxy body
lying in the coffin demanding all your heart? Mere man?
Or was it what he said: that we are the stuff of stuff
once dead, so why so much pettiness now? That self is sin?
Oh Linda, he had self enough for all of us!
Has female love no pride? Spirit, you murmur? Spirits,
the doctor said. Ulcers. He could not digest bread.
Nor has he spirit to return, as we have done,
to the scene of the crime--where he coiled at our ear and hissed
that we should disregard the facts and live on love--
narcotic love! It kept us reeling all these years.
We owe it all to Uncle Ed.

What? Again grieving?
Is that like Daddy's girl? Rather, delight we have
the Old Man off our backs--nor are we likely now

to bear his kind again: The road is paved; this valley
has flood control. Our hearts are technically dated. We
may walk the dirt erect, your kisses all for me . . . .

But where did he take you, Linda? Why did your young hand
wriggle to his like a fish to a cave? What easy hours
swirled down that sink? What secrets were kissed into this palm?
I cannot bear your wonder, your eyes like silent flowers!

ALL OUTDOORS

Hey look now I'm going to open the windows
and splash my face in winter air. Listen:
birds like squeaky springs. Listen: the hack
of axes. Feel: it warms its fingers in
my hair. The sun is a flashlight straining through
a curtain. The trees are cable frayed. Grass shreds
like old cigars. Look at the frost: lime spilled
on the fence posts. The pump has a tooth of ice.
The cows are standing smoking in their sheds.

The room turns inside out. My teeth are breaking.
The mirror clouds: Nothing *here* to see,
it says. Cabbage sweats from the woodwork. Laundry
stiffens in the hamper. The clock is breathing thinner,
the windows all have water in their eyes.
The stairs hunch darkly, cracking in their treads.

That mood which faced me shaggily across
the steamy bathroom sink is gone: all lies--
I knew it.
          Objective birds, sing off your heads.

APOLOGY FOR BAD BEHAVIOR

Blame not the wine. No grape as yet
has smeared with purple etiquette.
Blame not the night--for though dark dwells
in pools of lust, it never compels.
Blame not the season, moon, nor sea.
Blame not your beauty, nor my flesh. Blame me.

Dream of a blameless world where men
weed gardens of each sprouting yen,
committing naught but sober acts
with reverence for Right--and Facts.
Dream of that woman's world where no
dreaming hand travels where it should not go.

Then blame bad man, man even worse
if he loosens reason in a verse,
man shamed--who still finds strength to be
whatever you may love in me.
Blame me, love's liberal, who can
forgive (loosely) your *not* forgiving man.

THE GODDESSES

Taste

Like Justice, she is blind.
Also deaf, of palate numb,
sans olfactory capacity: Taste
is a matter of Mind.

She is trepanned,
an operation supposed
to open the Mind to God
(to all else, closed).

She speaks English
without gusto (without tongue, too!)
disputing with *chacun*
his own *gout*.

In myths she is the wife
of Money. Her symbol: scissors
(used to snip off Art
this side of Life).

She dominates one of the Temple's
marbliest halls
surrounded by posed favorites
offering balls.

Fact

Represented *flagrante delicto,*
she lies to please
any pilgrim prostrate
between her alabaster knees.

She has one head *per capita*
and rather average eyes
distributed around her nose
percentagewise.

These never close. She never dreams,
and never thinks nor jests.
She speaks only in headlines. In fact,
she doesn't speak--she screams.

(An oracle, her noises can
be interpreted by a Median,
a vested virgin, devotee,
reading riddles for her PhD.)

She reclines in an alcove, variously lighted.
The story goes, she is made of ice,
but will not melt unless a lover
foolishly looks twice.

Feeling

As you approach the shrine of Darkness
(where bespectacled penitents beg
forgiveness for reason and progress)
she looks rather like an egg,

turned in upon herself that way,
her ivory back to the fore,
arms clasped around her shins, her hair
tossed forward to the floor,

but what she finds, with her head in there,
her chin against her chest,
is the very yolk of wisdom:
body odor, manifest.

Daughter of Descartes (who took the form
of an ostrich to beget her,
then raped a loom in a factory,
which knitted her, like a sweater),

she gives to the touch, all love and blood,
archetypal, primitive, visionary.
(Some infidel scratched on her rump:
"Underage. Be wary.")

STONE MONKEY

I, archaeologist, unearthed
this limestone monkey clasping both
his shins and grinning with his chin
　　　　upon his knees.

What folk were these, who used a simian
measure of man and gods' dominion,
whose mind defined in squatting kind
　　　　divinities?

Where did (or *did?*) they draw the line
between such gods (or beasts) and sin-
ning humanness?　Twixt fur and skin
　　　　and stone, what fine

distinctions reconciled them to
their ease of imitating two
such natures:　mind and flesh combined,
　　　　beast and divine?

Do I, I pondered, leave such traces
of private fears in public places,
idols of gods I would be less
　　　　like if I could?

And do I worship memory
of what I fear I used to be
and save in stone my guilt outgrown,
　　　　revere the crude?

I noticed then the monkey's eyes
turned blankly angry at the skies.
The monkey smiled, but, smiling, lied:
　　　　resented what

it feared to fail to please. But gods
look *down,* or so I thought. What bodes
it if this joss attends a boss
        above, and not

our ceremonial dance, no more
concerned for us who set such store
by Him than monkeys, chins on knees,
        regard their fleas.

and under thunder absently pluck
the earnest of us when we suck,
devout dependents--thunderstruck?
        Oh, thoughts like these

make *me* return the monkey's stare,
glare at the pipsqueak god whose glare
is that of a beast who fears the fist
        of an outraged archaeologist!

A PACIFIST'S DILEMMA

If I were certain death were all,
I would die in war with fellow man--
for killing rightly should befall
men who, knowing killing, can,

but it *would* be Hell to wake and find
that after having justly crammed
into the maw my self and kind,
we had to live together--damned.

POLE VAULTING DOES NOT REQUIRE AN INDIVIDUAL STYLE

Except for personal adjustments
   their weight requires to fly,
their great endeavor is to conform
   their way into the sky,

with no waves to the audience,
   no tragic mien, or gay.
They do not seek to express themselves.
   They fling themselves away:

Grip, balance, run, and plant the pole,
   then catapult to space,
clearing the bar feet first to land
   with safety if not grace.

Poets can rarely clear the ground
   shouting *me* with all their might.
Pole vaulters have to save their breath.
   Their only point is height.

POETRY EDITOR AS MISS LONELYHEARTS

Round the horizon I see silhouettes
of sweet old ladies who live with their pets,
parents neglected by their children, scholars
bullied by schoolmates, men in starchy collars
whose daily wisdom always falls among swine,

girls who read on Saturday night, fine wine
merchants, inmates, shut-ins, neglected wives.
Love is a seller's market. Hope arrives
in bundles on my desk, these poems blest
with kisses, tears, stamped envelopes--self-addressed.

REJECTION SLIPS

What do you mean, More? Shall I
send fingers? I have a total of ten.
What do you mean, Good Work? That's my left eye!

Listen, you. Wait. Just when
we've had one moment only the two of us know,
what do you mean, Sorry? Try *what* again?

(I will poison the gum on my return envelope.) So
am I, oh editor, overstocked, but I,
when one comes, can never tell it No.

YOU HAVE TO TOOT YOUR OWN HORN
(to be sung to the tune of Yankee Doodle)

The flesh is weak: You need a bra
  to amplify your sweater--
and though I like the smell of you,
  I do like Lifebuoy better.

Truth is never enough: The act
  of love requires some acting.
One's friends are liars; enemies are
  sufficiently exacting.

Flatter as ye would be flattered;
  kiss as ye would be kissed.
I'd rather never go to bed
  than with a realist.

I find you as you say you are,
  complete in all essentials,
but be for me the apogee--
  and never mind credentials.

Don't hide your talent: Goods are good
  only when you sell them.
How can your customers know what
  they've bought, unless you tell them?

It pays to advertise. Think big.
  Eat grass, but call it clover.
Consider Jesus, Son of God.
  He nearly put it over!

CLAY

Give it *self*. Tear off a chunk and pound.
Hand heat and pressure make it round. It? Round?

It. Round. For every squeeze an opposite
impression comes from you and makes it it.

So shape is negative, but fat and real,
and regular if turned upon a wheel.

Turned? Rather, though your foot impels below,
it seems to *turn*. You hold--and it would *go*.

You educate it merely, thin it down,
as verbally it spins into a noun:

a pot, a thing in space, with out and in
you gave it. You. Your hands and discipline.

The clay is damp and finely granular,
less pliable than you, and yet you are

except for *some*thing, like this clay, this pot,
a self imposed on nothing, shaped from not,

defined, a hunk of motion with a name,
for every pot you make, not quite the same.

OIL OF THE PECOS VALLEY

In that kind of country even the yellowest blossoms
have thorns: Spring is just rattlers coming to water.
Dusters sweep down, and bulging clouds hurl hail.
Nature is sparing of green in the time of blossoms.

Buttes are the rock-heads, knuckles of world left bare,
impassively purple, rock-shrouded, sparing of soil.
That kind of country wears its hard-husked people
as goats wear drilling fleas in scanty hair.

The Pecos is salty, wriggly, threading, absurd
to have caused that country, worm of so empty a valley,
to have carried such acres of rock, in green running, away.
The first million years were likely the most absurd,

until, in its gully, indifferent, reluctantly fertile,
it ran more like plasma than blood, like lymph in the land,
colder than night in the night, colder in sunlight,
slick under bluffs, greener than thorn trees, and while

rabbits drink elsewhere, cedars absorb it, and cottonwoods,
continuously quivering, turn it to pulp and pale green.
The Pecos has only the sky in its sky and the sheen
of oil on its running on rocks under shuddering cottonwoods,

oil seeping from jungles, rotted, sunk under seas,
draining old liberalities of fern and of flesh,
seeping, now, into the Pecos--oil that is nurture
for nothing but people--sole nurture for these.

OTTER POINT, MAINE

More than a mile from the nearest rutted lane
was this spruce-tangled tip of granite knob
where life had given maybe fifty feet
to the chewing of the sea--and God knows when
if ever otter might have been there. Snails
dot all the tide fringe, and the million crusty-lidded
eyes of barnacles, eyeless starfish, stalk-eyed crabs.

Perhaps a nervous squirrel looked out where sails
passed pregnantly--the only human hint,
until blond pioneers, our Marj and Jim,
hewed passage for their yellow Model A,
which coughed and ground out, stubborn, to life's rim.
They liked that fog-soaked view and straightway built
a camp: hauled lumber over the roots, rocks, past the snails,

the bristling trees, and agonized the air
with saws and hammering. A measured, flat
floor then imposed its reason on the tough
and twisted wild. Beams diagrammed the sky.
Now brandy, stove, and window give the lie
to waves crumbling cold, dropping like scarves,
futile as instinct breaking upon the mind's rebuff.

FORCED LANDING

His engine failed in the air,
but when in a farm field one
wing touched, and, recovering,
he stalled, then nosed in hard,
it was the earth which snagged him, not the air.

And though at landing he
was able, ready, even
anxious to slip down soon,
we never like to see
one forced: The forces seem to be

so tough to skill and will.
He must have crumpled angry,
with loose controls, speed sagging,
dumping absurd in the field,
not to have poured--and then to spill.

We honor as we can:
No steady engine could
have eased his lonely landing,
have borne his private pain.
Air fails us when force spills a man.

MEMORIAL DAY

The Legion organizes a parade
with Boy Scouts, bands, the hardware man on a horse,
a float made on the lumber truck, a paid
clown from the city (other days a shoe-

salesman), the daughter of the druggist, wearing
lipstick and spinning a baton. All, all
is ceremonious, paraders staring
formally ahead as though quite unaware

of clusters at each corner of their friends
and enemies and families and children
(saluting every flag). Each one pretends
to be remembering whatever this

Sunday is special for, and thus the town
attends. A beanbake follows, proceeds for
the Presbyterians. And the sun goes down
long after Legionaires in undershirts

are settled by the set at home with beer
in artificial dark. The birds are loud
in mornings, now, and lawns begin to rear
their bristling backs: Dandelions yawn and stare.

A bother, spring, which still responds
to sacrifices made so long before
and still returns, although in these small towns
we hardly seem to need it any more.

THE NEGRESS IN THE CLOSET

That wise albino, flat of eye,
would poke the fire on Sunday afternoons,
lean on the mahogany mantle, his muscled lips
issuing polysyllables soft as blooms--
and I would nod to mind so seasoned
by suffering and solitude.

His bad foot scraped, his hump swayed,
as he reasoned like a mole from *is* to *should*
in his stately room of books, with bed like a bier,
deep leather chairs, brass smoking stand,
scent of orange tea, a portrait of Voltaire.
Civilized, I would shake his tender hand

and never stayed to see beneath his jacket
the braces and pale drum of bent spine,
white lashes blinking, free of spectacles,
or how he assisted his limp leg into line
between fresh sheets, then switched off
the last low lamp, or see the eyes

like spots of dominoes look from the closet,
the silhouette slip into bed to ease
that wise albino. I never visited
on Sunday mornings when this sturdy girl
slumped dark in her smock among stale coffee and papers,
her breath of loam engaged in monosyllabic quarrel.

ELEGY: BAREFOOT BOY

Lead soldiers once were lead, oh barefoot boy.
You sympathized with Ethiopians,
and Germans (in your mind confused with germs)
toppled in trenches in your garden wars,
but years, Spitfires and Messerschmitts made your
dirt digging and your tanks all obsolete.
Dive bombers dived to noises in your throat.
They rationed shoes right off your grateful feet.

A lock of hair pulled down, a comb upon
your lips, you made Sieg Heils into the mirror,
saved grease and hangers, paper, fingered a V,
and sang the notes Beethoven wrote to show
support of Churchill and the Allied Powers.
Air wardens were your generals when, unwary,
you smiled into a birthday and were taken,
nor wondered if the trip were necessary.

Children will play you with your quaint devices,
your GI boots and nylon parachutes.
Though jets outdate you, children will remember
some of the names of some of your enemies,
and though the name of Iwo or of Anzio
become a crossword, death become a toy,
and beaches wash themselves of leaden soldiers,
children will play you hard, oh barefoot boy.

PLEXUS AND NEXUS

I can prove who I am. I draw my wallet like
a six-gun. Look what all these numbers show:
core, corpse, corpuscle in many systems. Stopped,
I see in the mirror an upturned radio.

That tall young nun studies the mirror daily
learning to show emotion on her face.
That black boy sits in the darkness staring at
the image in the mirror of his race.

But I with light and sticky step may travel
the web of the world, springing the tense strands,
sensing the signals at each intersection,
darting the way my heart (it seems) commands.

I am the fly in the network and the network.
I exist at many levels, if at all.
I am the thousand images receding
in every surface of the mirrored hall.
I diffuse at the speed of light.
                                    Remember me!
the honest ghost, the wave, pulse, the fleet shape
imprinted on and by all I have met.

Experience runs through me like a tape.

1964-1968

"Jonah," written on St. Thomas, reflects my divided spirit
in those years. I am glad I was able to laugh at it. Marty and
I had four daughters--and briefly five. Twins were born prematurely, but only Jenny survived. She is the heroine of "Naughty
Little Witch!"--written when she was a baby. After we returned
to Ohio in 1965 we learned bit-by-bit that she had been severely
damaged--diagnosed eventually as aphasic, epileptic, with some
cerebral palsy. Our fifth (and last) child, Topher, was born in
1966.

We experienced culture-shock when we returned to find Antioch
infested with a breed of young people unknown to us. The college
and, indeed, that professional life into which I had become locked,
seemed to be falling apart. I became involved along with my
children. I remember Beth trying to explain to me "Eleanor Rigby."
I felt very much like the professor at the end of "A Decade of
American Poetry," clearing my throat. I was on the staff at
Bread Loaf Writers' Conference in 1967 and 1968--orgiastic experiences which further loosened the fibre of my life. I had become
a radical educator--especially after my article, "The System Really
Isn't Working," appeared in *Life* in 1968. The first seven of the
'Rumors of Change" were written in the fall of that watershed year.
(I have included the whole series in this section, though the
poems from "Middle Ages" on, written in 1977-78 for *The Green
Revolution,* are postscripts to a revolution which, after blast-off,
subsided to the pad.)

I had quit the Department of Literature--symbolically and
actually. I had given up classroom teaching and considered myself
Professor at Large (a term I was defining). Marty and I were
playing high-stake poker several nights a week. Village and
campus were heavy with controversy. We were tense and torn, but
was almost giddy with release from the spiritual doldrums
f the past decade.

ST. THOMAS SUITE
(1964)

January

No glass on the windows. All winter the air
tickled our torsos, tactile as talcum,
or moaned in the jalousies, maniacally gusting
as the East emptied its air on our islands,
whipping our palm fronds, whirling my papers,
obliterating thought, blowing it westward.

Our porch like a prow, imperiously eastward,
is seared by the sunshine, receives the full wind
from the Atlantic which lashes low Anegada,
flattens the Fat Virgin, furrows Tortola,
scours St. John in sunwash and windwash
to ream St. Thomas as it tumbles westward,
building on the golfcourse, galing down the airstrip
(we receive all the earsplit of aircraft on takeoff)
to pummel our porch. Then Puerto Rico gets it.

Our metal chairs screechingly skid down the concrete
in this buffet of weather, the wailing of January.
I stand out there naked, needled by gold sun,
slapped by the blue beat of sky and of sea,
of endless Caribbean, achingly empty,
seeing St. Croix shadowy to the South,
westward the low loaves of larger Antilles,
sailing my boxkite (which snaps on its cord)
in the vortex (I think), vacantly brilliant,
of world winds, of tempests, equatorial eddies,
standing white in the blaze of the banging blue winter,
standing skinny and timid in time's torrid zone.

May

This May was browner than a March in Boston.
The golfcourse crisped by winter drouth is dead
as a snowfield cleared by thaw. When the planes drone
over the smoking garbage dump toward San Juan,
their wings seem limp. The flamboyant in the yard

rattles its two-foot pods and puts forth sprigs
of weary ferny green. The calendar reads Spring.
Our volcanic rubble and crumbled coral collect
little water, no streams, no lakes. A scrub spreads
on the dry hills--grey, green, durable as fact.

This parched south side is thorny, tough, cluttered
with traffic and slums. A highway severs the tattered
tin and concrete buildings, car bodies, rubbish.
No house is inhabited as though it mattered.
No home embodies a memory or wish.

We are campers, as were the Arawaks and Caribs
or Spaniards, English, Africans, or Danes.
Native, maybe, are lizards, sandflies and crabs.
Mongooses are imported. We pitch shelters on slabs,
fill the air with chopping copters, creaking cranes.

The steeper north side stops the rain, and jungle
infects its pockets, inflamed with flowers, a tangle
succulent, humming, dank. Roots feed on thick air.
The French grow bananas. On misty cliffs mingle
colonial aristocrats of yesteryear.

A rainbow of flags has shimmered above St. Thomas,
leaving no imprint as it drifted away in the sun.
Now no land tilled, fish caught, orchards tended,
no epic or song, no name goes from father to son.
Dark blurs all seasons, nations, dreams, and tongues.

I camp here in former officer's quarters, unwilling
to join either the pirates or slaves, even failing
to teach the slaves to be pirates, the black to be white.
Day after day the pirates go fishing and sailing.
I tell my students of Spring in the sunsoaked night.

September

Grace (the hurricane) passed safely to the North
and here we sit becalmed, culture becalmed.
Tortola sloops churn forth,

sails slopping round their knees. Sun-numbed,
the lake of sea licks at our vacant beaches.
Our air is enclosed, steel-drummed.

I sit still, very still. My skin itches.
Insects settle on the shacks in valleys.
The rich sweat in high niches.

And, as was bound to happen eventually,
thought has, like a truck in sand, ground to a stop,
hubs under, *sans finale*.

Now nuns mumble Latin as on an endless tape
to classes learning never to lift their chins.
Gobs drink themselves shipshape.

Taxis, like logjammed sharks fin to fin,
clog Main Street, bellow an eternal dying honk.
Pink patrons taken in

by gift shops never emerge. They gawk blank
(in ballooning shorts and floral hats) at clerks
who glare back blackly blank.

184

Impasse. Outage. They abandoned Public Works,
and all our goods are now tied up in Customs.
            The Coastguard offshore lurks

to intercept incoming mail. Boat bums
bail yachts awash in rum (for we lack water).
            See: a thirsty fag succumbs.

Late *Daily News* say the news he soon be later.
The College offers an evening course in how
            to communicate with a waiter.

This pot has melted. A dirge in Calypso
makes a dirty joke of the waste of the human race.
            Wherever tourists go

in the lee of missions and commerce they erase
before they can impose. The Fall is slow.
            I itch in the lee of Grace.

December

Before dawn came the change: Our sheet billowed, we snuggled as one.
Outside a black wind had blown clouds off the shivering stars.
Seventy-two is no joke! All new air and a corn-yellow sun.
Our daughters all chattered. The hills hunched like cold dinosaurs.
Professorial, I hiked through the bush thinking *football* and *tweed*.
I heard Hope cry to me from the College. My heart answered Love!

I had answers that morning, feeling the tropics recede
from the goose-pimpled sea and naked blue gospel above.
My St. Thomas stupor, like autumn, was gone, my wits sleek.
Students huddled in sweaters. Our tank of a classroom (flourescent)
holds St. Kitts and Antigua, Dominica, New Jersey, Martinique--
a dusky-toned Council of Nations (most post-adolescent).

First, a question from Carmen: Crucian lilt and the vowels of Spain.
Shy Annette makes a guess in Tortola's marshmallow patois.
My dark Chaplin (Charles), moustached, and stiffly urbane,
who as clerk for the Crown in Barbados learned language and law,
gives the point-of-view of a Christian accountant (mistaken).
Knowledge spreads like a stain in the room, like shame upon joy.

They toil through sand-drifts of words like Magi forsaken.
We piece together New York as one reconstructs Troy.
I describe the World (shrinking), the Universe (expanding),
tell how cultures barbarously born grow to genteel decay.
I talk to myself. They take notes on their misunderstanding.
Our hearts are in touch, our minds flying starlike away.

Now the jalousies whine, rain whips us and passes, we swear
at the frizzled firs brought us from Canada, traffic crawls
as tourists unload, Christmas avarice sharpens the air.
Creaking yachts rock at anchor or fly before sudden squalls.
We string lights over coral and conch shells, address UN cards,
lie sunbaked on beaches with beer while the radio tells

us of Rudolph, of blizzards, prizefighting, low Commie canards,
of the Congo, of Buddhists in flame, and then Jingle Bells.
Under palms in the park a white overdressed Santa's laugh rings
as black waifs stand in line for his promises, candies, and squeezes.
Amahl at the highschool is black, as are all three kings.
They sing softly offkey of the magic of white baby Jesus.

For our four pale northern and fairheaded flowers we wrap
oil, frankincense, myrrh, from that India now known as Sears,
our season of peace in a world that is cocked as a trap.
Shall we shiver a lifetime remembering tropical years?
Silent night! On the porch with a drink we sit nude under stars
to celebrate peace and survival. We look for a sign

such as Mariner IV, which is racing the Russians for Mars.
Yet in spite of all human endeavor, the earth seems benign.
Our dot of an island is rosy with Cha-cha and rum,
surrounded by phosphorous sea and black taffeta night.
Merry Christmas! we shout to Old Nick, and stand till we're numb,
staring long, darkly North, where his empty sleigh sank out of sight.

THE BARGAIN

Be beautiful as you are, and for
    wit winking electric and your patience that
        contains our family like a shore,
your tilted bones, your circular day
    tending a household which, like a pile of fish,
        needs perpetual putting away,
or, getting pound per ounce,
    threading your spirit endlessly to patch
        our metaphysical accounts,
yet leaping at dawn from the bed's warm pool,
    landing on sand and flopping on to get
        dozens of daughters off to school,
remain receptive as an eye,
    enduring and softly holding as a glove
        which I completely occupy
reliably as a nightlight glow,
    and every other day I'll take out garbage
        and say again each decade or so
in a poem, awkward, inexact,
    how I am wealthier than all professors
        for having made this lucky pact.

THE NAP

Sinking in ether buzz on a hot day,
all bare and brown on the sheet like a long boy,
my bosomy pillow warmed by breath, I lay
in lattice of limber muscle, drifting in joy,
when talons blazed their hooks in shoulder meat
with the crush of a vulture pouncing, taking hold,
awkwardly cruel, rocking in black, foul heat--
this thought: *I am damned near forty years old.*

Well, after an hour of typing some drivel as though
I could stitch up a paper defense, a scarecrow for Time,
I looked in the mirror, but found no stigmata, no
blood, few grey hairs--and the grin of a man in his prime.
  But, Milton, those whose light is sputtering nerve--
  a fuse with no bomb at the end--do they also serve?

YOGURT IS NOT ENOUGH

As a nail-keg seasoned to a silver sheen
stands by a winter shed and gently caves
into the earth, the hardened mulch of summer
bulging at seams between its spreading staves,
so does my trunk, ending its fortieth year,

strain to contain within its hoop of belt
the indigestible richness it has garnered,
holding together till its contents melt.
Yogurt is not enough--nor games of squash--
to counteract indiscipline of age.

I see why the old hate other people's pleasures
and hate their flesh which eggs them to engage.

JONAH

I

In which the pathetic circumstances of Jonah's upbringing and
education are related, along with his discovery of his intuitive
understanding of absolute truth, his general superiority to his
fellow man, and his disgust with a world which is too good for
most people and not good enough for him.

Jonah woke to street cries, not to bird songs.

Jonah took no joy in the games of his playmates.
   He listened for the Lord's voice in the hush of the temple.
   He lingered with his teachers. With books he dwelt.

And it came as nausea in the midst of feasting:
   My teachers are not exalted, and their wives weep.
   Narrow is their vision. Their wisdom is wine-washed.

It came on the bright streets ugly and clamorous:
   in the market--worship; in the temple--trade.
   Lo, the beggar is not humble; he counts coin.

In the midst of gatherings, in the smoke of the city
   to the young Jonah, on the wires of his nerves,
   the Lord said *rotten,* and the Lord said *false.*

At dawn at the wharves the great ships unloaded.
   The caravans, heavy, wound in through the gates.
   And Jonah was sleepless; Jonah was heartsick.

Speak, said the Lord--and Jonah was dumbstruck.
   Shall I speak in the schools, where truth is forbidden?
   Shall I speak in the temples, where evil is ignored?

How can I cry out? Your hurricane is upon us,
  and Your holocaust holds its breath only a moment.
    Shall I speak to the warlords, proud of their spears?

Who will publish Your truth, Lord? Who will be editor?
  Will they soil me with celebration? Will they award me a prize
    and feast me, and the women come and bring me wine?

Speak, said the Lord. *Speak My anger, My warning.*
  Jonah pondered at parties. In libraries he pondered.
    It is written--they read not. It is on their tongues--nor can
                                                  they hear.

Unshaven, Jonah walked in their places of business.
  Do they know the fields which feed them? Have they pressed oil?
    Which of these drinkers has handled the grape?

The grain bends and the orchards are heavy
  without their labor, and the cattle gestate upon the plains.
    The water of the hill darkly flows here in conduits.

Their maidens bear no baskets or jars on their shoulders.
  They bear papers and numbers; they copy words.
    Never do I see them beating clothes by the river.

Their warriors in the taverns laugh with the harlots,
  and sailors whistle at youths on the docks.
    The young men have narrow shoulders and imported chariots.

The elders are not honored; they have no wisdom.
  They wear sweaters in summer, meddle and complain,
    and their sons dream of sending them off to warm climates.

Hungry, Jonah walked at dawn by the river.
  Have they seen Your sun, Lord? Have they considered Your stars?
    Your land is paved over. How may it support them?

They plant no seed, and yet their wagons groan.
They hunt not with arrows, yet their wives wear furs.
They watch no flocks: Meat is fat on their plates.

Jonah at mid-morning sat with the elders
on a bench under trees with his hands in his pockets.
Lo, the pigeons waddle. They neither fly nor hunt, but are fed.

And the Lord asked, *Do you well to be silent with your burden?*
Did I give you vision that it should drown only in your eyes?
Do you think their wickedness comes unto you, and I see it not?

Awaken them, Jonah. Speak out against profit.
And Jonah asked scornfully, Would You take that away?
What then would they live for? Do You think they would find You?

They would shrink, baffled, as a dog abused,
for profit is their love, and they love only for it.
Lo, they eat not with relish, but because one must eat to gain.

Which of them savors the meat or holds the fruit to the morning light?
Which of them says of his beloved: Behold! Behold!
They deck women with jewels that they may travel with rich men.

And the sons are fleet in games that their fathers may boast,
and the daughters kept chaste, that no shame befall.
For honor makes money; from shame comes little profit.

Does the craftsman feel the grain of the wood with his thumb
and love the odor of shavings, the fine steel of his saw?
Does he polish the strong joints in evening light?

Does the tailor stitch the seam firmly, though no one will see?
Does the butcher arrange red meat in loving display?
Which carter knows the underside of his cart?

Nay, but the merchant knows not his wares nor the feel of his fabric.
He sits in the back room, and girls bear his messages.
His cigar ash drops on the carpet; he reads market reports.

Does that poet love words? Nay, he loves reputation.
Does the scholar love learning? Nay, security.
See the saintly priest seeking a larger parish.

And I tell You, Lord, as sure as the stone falls and the smoke drifts
upward,
profit is the way of their hearts, and they know no other.
To say, Seek not profit is to say, Drink sand, Build with water.

And the Lord said, *Speak*.

II

*In which Jonah, a willing (and subsidized) exile, sets out a-hosteling
with faith that surely any other society is better than the one he
left; but he finds that he is the object of the Lord's attention--and
that a Lord stupidly generous to the common people is not above picking
on His own prophet.*

Jonah pitied the public and spoke not.

He applied for a fellowship, laughed that they gave it,
and fled their beneficence--and the presence of the Lord.
He took duffle to dockside and sailed off with foreigners.

At the bow lay Jonah, dipping in the salt spray,
parched by the sunbeat, chilled in the starlight,
his scarf flapping as they slipped through the plankton.

All night he listened, and the Lord was still.
He spoke not from the dark waves rolling under like elephants.
In the cold sky He was silent as it swayed above the spars.

Jonah laughed with the wind in his mouth,
for his appetite was returning, and his blood throbbed clean.
His skin hardened in the weather; his eyes sharpened.

The sailors were simple. Jonah loved the sailors,
their brown backs aloft, their dicing on the afterdeck.
The captain was bearded; Jonah let his own beard grow.

The Lord, he thought, is in the city, as one snared in webbing,
even as the spinner tangled in his own yarn
or the baker bound in by his oven's abundance.

The spare ship, economical, leans with the wind,
its sweet water rationed, its hard biscuits counted,
each line of its rigging named and in good repair.

I flee before the wind His excess and His bounty.
Surely my silence is holy, for I damn not what He has made.
Nor do I drink of His fermenting casks.

And the great ships, burgeoning, passed on the horizon,
swollen with produce, slipping down the tide,
drawn by the city, its bowels and its gutters.

Jonah swung on the ratlines and hailed ships in passing
as their light craft sped outward, Eastward, away.
God is wealthy, he cried. Go seek Him, and welcome!

He will reward with the bountiful gift of His hand.
The city shall prosper--and I shall escape it.
In the hold in his hammock he swung happily and slept.

But a sailor with lifted lantern was shaking him,
the bilge swirling at his ankles, the ship tossing.
Above, the wind screamed; as God were outraged, it screamed.

Around them the waves bulged mountainously, blackly,
and broke on the bow, flooding cargo and crew.
Jonah's hands were white as they gripped the wet rigging.

God of Outrage! he cried, and have You awakened?
Fling You fire at our mast? Do You shred our furled sails?
Have You thunder to blast me? Jonah howled with wet lips.

Lo, Your sea runs fiercely over the gunwales,
and Your wind flattens the sailor to the mast.
The bearded captain, arms locked in the wheel, mumbles prayers.

And cannot even one escape You? Has Your blind fury found me,
even on the Eastward sea, even on the trackless waves?
Do You bring adversity to me, who would flee Your gifts?

The prostrate sailors prayed to their gods,
each to his god, to many gods if they had them;
if they had none, they used gods of their shipmates.

They cried out to Jonah, whose lifted face, rain-dashed,
quarreled with the thunder, yelled into the cone of wind,
begging that he kneel, that his foreign god be propitiated.

For the sky split with fire, bellowing, bursting,
and its lips spoke a language electric, unintelligible.
Draw lots, they cried. The lot fell to Jonah.

Cast me over. He seeks me, for I fled His presence.
I bear His burden, His vision of evil.
I corrupt this vessel, Jonah shouted, defiant.

Who are you, voyager, who with glee greets the tempest?
One who refused to serve as God's fool.
Cast me forth, for I know things that men better not know.

But the captain pitied him. Until this ship founders
we will seek out some shore and abandon you there.
Then the ship broached; a wave fell like a tent of a Titan.

Cast me forth! Let my drowning be upon His head.

3

In which Jonah finds himself mighty thankful for a life for which
he couldn't care less.

Came Leviathan up from the depths like a cork.

Jonah was instantly breathing in silence,
nor did he hear the waves, nor pitch with the sea.
Walls of damp flesh closed him in, gripped him tightly.

Suffocating, he fainted, and his sleep was three days.
Pressure of water and darkness surrounding,
he lay curled in that belly, and in innocence lay.

Oh Lord, cried he, waking, cried voiceless but heartfelt,
in what depths do I travel? And how may I live?
As though tangled in weeds at the roots of mountains,

I lie strangled by intestines and suckled by salt.
Yet I thank You for dumb life, for my ignorant pulse continuing,
for the quickness of my flesh obliviously enduring.

And does Your breath reach even unto these dark places?
Do You stir life from the silt of the deep?
Does this salt quicken, this water render air to me?

Mindless the multiplication of fish beneath the light
and weeds on the twilight shelves of the sea's blue ranges.
You are indifferently abundant, Your pockets spilling.

Have You reached even in the black water, even to this belly?
And even to the atoms of my cramped body, to each and all
have You brought sustenance? And may I eat

at the table of life, even here in my despair?
What am I that in these coral catacombs
Your casual chemistry should sustain me, and my soul answer You?

For the great fish swallows the small and swallows me
without regard, and the weeds at my wrist whisper upwards
without gratitude or fear, but I, with the gift

to know my condition, the gift to suffer,
contend with You in dialogue. You know I am here.
Even in the primal slime and belly juices

I bear Your burden. I know Your intolerable goodness.
I am glutted by Your wealth and may not relinquish
knowledge You have given me to torment my flesh.

Had I my life as a feather in my hand,
I could not release it; I could not blow it on the air.
You have bound me to be, and to witness Your absurdity.

For my deliverance, thank You, oh Lord.

IV

*In which Jonah finally stoops to publish his most violent and holy
feelings--and finds success more repugnant than failure.*

The fish vomited.

Jonah walked clothed from the sea among the bathers.
Young, brown bodies around him paused in their play.
Some looked through glasses darkly, under gay parasols.

And on the horizon gleamed the tall buildings,
  the sun glaring on the city, the sprawl of the millions.
  Tell them, said the Lord. *Tell them I sent you.*

Vexed, then, and reckless, Jonah spoke at the crossroads
  and the market, the assembly hall, in all public ways.
  His book he sullenly delivered, and the people read it eagerly.

Fathers gave it to sons and swains to their sweethearts.
  The rulers of the city read and discussed it, and the ministers also.
  The scholars required their disciples to study it,

and Jonah was appalled, for they read and believed.
  It spoke of the hour of the empire's destruction,
  of life lived for nothing, waste, wickedness, lies.

And lo, over the city came a great transformation:
  As when garments are cut in a new way, and the great ones wear them,
  and soon in every street are seen only garments cut that way,

so goodness and love spread over the city, from the rulers
  to the beggars; nay, even to the carters and militia.
  They clothed themselves in fashionable sackcloth and blessed the Lord

The temple was crowded, the market honest.
  Jonah saw the streets empty in the evening and families at the hearth.
  Yea, they went early to bed and gardened on weekends.

Jonah, disgusted, banged on the tavern door to no avail.
  Do you conform to new laws as to any other?
  Do you indulge in virtue as once you indulged in vice?

And have you tarnished charity by making it your goodness?
  For he who competes in goodness to shame his brother,
  who uses charity to store alms in Heaven,

seeks profit of God. He soils all that is sacred.
  And do you fear the fall of empire, and so repent?
  Ah, how desperately you cling to your goods and your city!

I see the young men laboring and the maidens kind to their mothers,
  the elders revered, nay, even the cattle tended kindly.
  Your garments are washed and the gutters of the city sparkle.

Thrift has descended upon you as a kind of paralysis.
  The merchants put up modest announcements. The police take no bribes.
  Yea, those of high place are returning money to the public coffers.

How tedious such virtue! How docile! How conventional!
  Have I chastized your stagnation that you may discover complacency?
  Ah, with what relief you avoid error!

How eagerly you seek the safety of reason, the haven of justice!
  You teach your children, Traffic not with evil,
    and their hearts wither, and their minds grow dull.

But the lord looked benignly on the city and filled its warehouses.
  The hospitals emptied, and the walls of the city were strong.
    Blessed be the city, said the Lord. The city prayed thanksgiving.

Jonah turned up his collar, set out gloomily across desert sands.

                              V

*In which Jonah believes the Lord at last sees Jonah's point-of-view
but is disappointed in Him when He relapses into His profligate ways.*

On one hand blue mountains, on the other buildings of glass and stone.

Here Jonah in the wasteland: Oh Lord, Your reward falls
  as rain after long drouth, indifferently to good and bad;
    to the thirsty it falls, and to the drowning;

on the living and on the crisp corpse. The stupidly evil city You
                                                   threaten,
and You bless the city, reformed without understanding.
The dungheap feeds the rose, and all is blessed.

Why should I then have spoken? Would You have them laugh,
saying, See, Jonah cries doom upon us, and the doom falls not?
Is it sackcloth that raises such pity in Your heart?

Do You think they are virtuous for love of You or of virtue?
Nay, Lord, but in prudence, in fear for their lives they are good,
and, worse, in fear of their neighbor's opinion.

Do You think they fear the terror of the Lord? Nay, oh Lord.
They fear the foreigner and him of another color,
and strive to excel that they be not shaken.

Worse, they are as plants choking the tropical jungle, exuberant,
or as the improvident plant that grows between cobbles of the
                                                   street.
Water them, they flourish; tread on them, they learn not.

If they may prosper by virtue, they adopt virtue.
Do they abandon the harlot to love their wives and children?
Nay, for fear of disease, impotence, to save money, they
                                                 abandon her.

They risk nothing for pleasure. They risk nothing to serve in Your
                                                 name.
See their empire spreading its wealth among the poor and ignorant.
As one dreads hungry beasts, they feed the clamoring nations.

Their homes are full of delicate music and difficult books,
for, verily, they seek thus to put their neighbors to shame.
The poor are given clean houses that the price of land not fall.

See the scrubbed schoolboy carrying books to a school with many
windows.
Thus the father is not shamed; the mother need not tend her young.
He learns to obey without question, and his questions are silenced.

Should I then have spoken? You are too easily pleased, oh Lord,
to bless goodness that is a surrender, not a struggle.
Was I honoring You, revealing thus Your dotage?

In the dry desert air Jonah wept in anger.
When the sun burned him, and the drouth parched his throat,
when the sand whipped his face, he felt pure.

A false step here means death. Here one must fear God's power.
In the fierce sun and shimmering light must he fear Him.
The desert is just and allows no waste of water.

The sandals of Jonah burned his feet, and his skin flaked.
Here I sit where the distant city stains the sky.
Here in the sterile sand I await the Lord's judgment.

Surely, seeing me a witness for truth, He will not ignore me.
No profit seek I here, nor pleasure; I seek reasonable treatment.
He will see my patience and see how little man needs.

Nor will He reward me with cattle and green things of His bounty,
for then my goodness would be venal, my protest spoiled.
But he will bring down the city; it will fall in a heap before me.

He will cut the city from the earth as a sore, with a clean knife.
He will confound the masses and crush the power elite,
and perhaps may restrain His creativity hereafter.

As a sign there grew beside Jonah a great gourd.
In a day it grew, and its broad leaves made shade.
In the desert sand it found sustenance, in the baked air moisture.

Blessed be the chemistry of life, said Jonah.
As in the salt sea, so in these shifting sands is there nurture.
Blessed be God for this gourd, to shade my vigil.

How rational, oh Lord, to provide a single gourd where shade is
needed.
Do You not delight in the justice of sensible planning?
Do You not repent all that has spilled from Your prodigal hand?

And the Lord then provided a worm from His womb that is never dry.
The gourd is good food for worms, so the Lord made a worm.
In a day the worm ate, and the gourd withered.

And God sent a sultry East wind bearing no relief, but the odor of
garbage.
The heat of the sand it bore, and the city's foul stench.
The limp stem of the plant lay across Jonah's lap, and he wept.

In anger and despair he wept, crying upon the Lord for death.
Have You no mercy for the lone and stalwart gourd
in the midst of adversity, testifying to Your power,

growing without loam, without the dew or rain growing?
After all Your beneficence, had You no mercy for my gourd?
Look: Even the worm dies. He is fat and cannot find shelter.

And the Lord, who is a patient Lord, but was somewhat weary of Jonah,
asked, *Would you have Me save this gourd*
and bring the city down, with all its people and cattle?

Is that economy? If they know not their right hand from their left,
should I therefore condemn them, even as the innocent gourd?
Do you resent the latitude of my mercy

who in the entrails of the fish found air, and are tolerated
even upon these yellow sands in the heat of the sun?
Is it you who would found the world on logic?

And now would you choose to die? Would my lecturer die?
Nay, speak to the people a sequel. Say God is no computer.
Complain of that in the tavern, for already the tavern is opening.

Jonah went, thirsting for unreason, and his heart was not at peace.

HELIUM: AN INERT GAS

My ego, like a pink balloon,
  bobs on a string behind
or floats above me where I sit--
  self-effacing, kind.

Sometimes I hug it to my chest
  getting in and out of cars
or ask my friends to hold it for me,
  especially in bars.

My boss says keep it out of sight
  in the kneehole of my desk.
In traffic, how it dances, jerks
  in nervous arabesque!

I should not bring it to the table,
  but when I come, it comes,
though kids giggle and point at it
  and pummel it with crumbs.

Sometimes I dream it drifts away
  above the curling sea,
though it is safely under the sheet
  between my wife and me.

My doctor, friends, and family
  all wonder what's inside.
I think they'd like to pop it, watch
  it flabbily subside.

NAUGHTY LITTLE WITCH!

The Way to the Witches' Home

On the road that winds
  through Crossbone Woods
    the traveler finds
      (if he's very brave)
        three rotting scarecrows
      dressed in hoods
    right at the corner
  by Gruesome Grave.
    Observe the arrows
      that point to the left.
        These you must follow
        through Foggy Hollow
      till you come to the cave
    cut in the cleft
  of Dead Man Bluff.
    The door is draped
      with a spider-web curtain.
                    Knock.
                    Speak rough.

(And do be certain
your feet are scraped
before you go inside.
While these witches won't *refuse*
visitors with muddy shoes,
many have mysteriously
died.)

Mother Witch

The lady of the house is kind old Mother Witch,
with her eyes like sores and her mouth like a ditch.
Her husband, a warlock, loves his wife dearly,
though he shows his love a little bit queerly.

He kicked out her teeth to string them for pearls--
a Halloween gift for their four little girls.
He visits home monthly, beats his wife with a stave,
then leaves--after paying the rent on the cave.

With a bone for a needle, Mother sews a fine stitch
to make capes out of cobwebs for each little witch.
She has a black cat, which she named You Rat!
and a tall black hat made from skin of a bat.
She rides on a broom with a bicycle seat,
and a strange apparatus for resting her feet.
She boils a thick broth of moss, toads and cockroaches.
Its aroma knocks out anyone who approaches.

Though she has little beauty, less wit, fewer riches,
she raises her daughters to be good little witches.

Grisly

Who is that whose
bed's a coffin?
Drinks her broth from
baby skulls? It's
Mother Witch's
eldest daughter,
Grisly, as the
girls all call her,
Ghostly Grisly,
Graveyard Grisly,
daughter of the
stagnant marshes,
child of wormy
earth and spiders.

At her birth she
did not cry but
hooted, rather,
spooky, kooky.
As her pet she
keeps a vulture,
trains him how to
follow funerals,
feeds him fillets of
former witches.
(For herself she
saves the gristle.)
Children scream when
Grisly visits.

Drizzly

When you hear a howl
and a sniffling scold
from a witch who looks
like an owl with a cold,

it is probably Drizzly,
the second sad daughter.
(Mother Witch poisoned
the stork which brought her.)

A fat little witch,
she splits clothes to rags.
When she goes aloft
her broomstick sags.

Her skin is white
as mashed potatoes,
her eyes as red
as sliced tomatoes.

Speak nicely to her:
She seems to hate it.
She had a pet rabbit,
but she ate it.

Drizzly visits near and far
each day of the calendar
leaving tempers and tears
as souvenirs.

Brat

When you hear a great crash of pottery
and run out to the kitchen in nothing flat
and see *no one* (though the cupboard is open and one plate still
                                                          tottery)
but the shadow of someone fleeing like an acrobat--
                    that
                    was Brat.

When everything is peaceful on a Sunday afternoon,
then the cat screeches as though she had sat in hot fat,
and the baby in the playpen is making a strange noise
                          like a submerged bassoon,
and the floor is littered with clothes, books, toys and such as that,
                    you know Brat
                    has come--and scat.

She's a cute little witch when you see her--
red pigtails and freckles and a dimple in her chin--
but when she takes a notion to go on a spree, her
angelic smile becomes a devilish grin,

then she puts on her pistols and her cowboy hat,
mounts her broom with her lariat,
and thunders away--pit-a-pat, pit-a-pat--
until from the distance comes a great loud *SPLAT!*
                              That
                          was Brat!

Irma

Grisly and Drizzly and Brat are *good* witches,
        the pride of their mother's heart,
but their tiniest sister is a *naughty* little witch
        who failed to learn her part.

When she was a baby you never could call her
        a mother witch's dream.
Why, when Irma, in her cradle, saw her first ghost,
        she let out a bloody scream!

She lacks Grisly's love of the monstrous
and Drizzly's love of the mean
and Brat's love of the mischievous.
She has a strange desire to be clean.

She thinks cow's milk is better than bat's milk for babies,
        that a broom is something to sweep with,
that cats squalling at the moon make a horrible tune--
        and a rat is a strange thing to sleep with.

When her family at night goes to cause people fright
        and misery, bother, and itches,
Irma stays in the cave, sees them off with a wave--
        then plays pranks.
                    But she plays them on witches!

Her tall black hat looks funny
sitting on her yellow curls,
and her laughter is sweet as honey--
not a cackle, like the other girls'--

> and her teeth won't snaggle,
> and her hair won't straggle,
> and her eyes don't glow in the dark,
> and her voice isn't screechy,
> and her cheeks look peachy.
> When she comes near, the dogs don't bark.

Though Irma is clearly a pitiful flop--
> as a witch, she hasn't the touch--
she sings as she plays, with a skip and a hop.
> It seems not to bother her much.
> > *Naughty little witch!*

Witches in the Morning

Good little witches sleep all day--
but that's when Irma likes to play.

When dawn comes, Mother starts to mutter,
bars the door, closes each shutter,

puts her broom in the closet with her tall black hat,
then curls in her gown like a weary bat.

Irma's sisters drop their toys--
such as knives, matches, worms (which a witch enjoys)--

and tuck their grimy little heads
into their ashcans--used for beds.

But Irma has the nasty habit
of hopping up then, like a rabbit,

checking Mom's and sisters' snores,
then tip-toeing out of doors

to hear the birds and sniff the flowers
and play with dolls for sunny hours.

Naughty little witch!

A Lesson in Manners

"The time has come," said Mother Witch,
 "You must learn to misbehave.
Go out and cut a thorny switch . . . .
 Your mommy has to shave."

Obedient Irma brought a switch
 and stood at Mommy's knees.
"Whoever heard of an obedient witch?"
 asked Mommy, scratching fleas.

"First, your grooming. Snarl your hair.
 Look angry, mean and wild!"
Poor Irma failed. Her silky hair
 just wouldn't knot. She smiled.

"Stick out your tongue and cross your eyes.
 That smile we have to squelch."
"I'm sorry, Mom."
 "Don't apologize!"
 said Mommy with a belch.

Unhappy that she failed to please,
 Irma began to weep.

"That's better!" cried Mom, and slapped her knees.
    "Now snivel like a creep!"

"Thank you, Mommy," Irma sniffed,
    glad she was catching on.
"Don't *thank* me. Don't thank *anyone*,"
    said Mommy, with a yawn.

Thus Irma learned to pout and whine
    and when to disobey--
but behind Mom's back, her face would shine,
    and her secret heart was gay.

                    Naughty little witch!

Witches in the Evening

When October comes the days grow short,
    and noses start to run,
for the air is chilled, and the sky is filled
    with clouds instead of sun.

When an evening gust stirs sheets of dust,
    driving children in from play,
then the shutters creak, and the floors all squeak,
    and windows are blankly grey,

and a dead leaf scrapes in the gutter like
    a skeleton's bony hand,
and a bat sweeps low, and a cawing crow
    makes music in the land,

and the dog has fits when the stray cat spits
    and her hair stands stiff as a brush,
as the darkness falls, and the black wind wails
    or dies with an eerie hush,

and the moon in a cloud seems a skull in a shroud
    making hazy, shifting light,
which the children watch from the window seat--
    and hold each other tight.

On such a night the witches' delight
    is to climb on their brooms and fly
with cackling laughter (till midnight or after)--
    black kites across the sky.

On such a night the witches' delight
    is to ride with the sheeted dead--
except for Irma, who
                much prefers to
    spend such nights in bed.
                    Naughty little witch!

THE SUPERIORITY OF MUSIC

Lang has no lovewedge. The world forgot
such courtly praise for neon eyes
as roused their hurricano sighs
in knightly years. I am not
like a yacht, nor dare I to
a harbor resemble thee. My tears
gully no landscapes. I have no fears
of chill disdain, nor wanly woo
pent in pantameter. My verse is ill
with marriage and commonsense
constraining conceit and elegance.
Shall I sonnetize the Pill?

Nay, wife, I still with clapper tongue
proclaim that you, like any she
belied with false compare, may be
with hyperbolic baubles hung:
I root my ropy route among
your petal hills; I pioneerly boar
my sow of despond, salty shore,
or, as spring from pikespeak sprung,
twist down melodically and clear.
I lick the jewels from corners, halt
midair nijinskywise, I sault
summerly and slobber, bucking near,

for you, my satin-saddle, gra-
vy grave, my scorching wine, my squirrel.
I love you like boiled onions, girl,
buttered. You suck my spine away,
soak me. You tenderize my twigs.
I think in orange. My tongue twitches

till sundown. You invent my itches.
You look like music and taste like figs.
You are to be virtuo-solely played,
sweetly and with pizzicato,
ad libitum and obbligato,
my straddle-various, my fiddled maid.

No go. The mind in praise ties knots.
Yet when you lie there like a long smile
brownly smiling at either end a long while,
moon glazing your gullied landscape, thoughts
circling and settling like evening birds,
and you turn and stroke my skin with eyes
like tonic chords, and silence lies
as gently over us as music without words,
I would not then restore to love its tongue.
You are not like anything. No poet imagined you.
You are dreamed by the earth, wordless. You
are not to be described, but sung.

WAVE,

not water but of water . . . not form
    but form in motion . . . changing
        as variation on a norm . . .
            as self through unself ranging . . .

impinging forces . . . wind, world rotation,
    moon pull and river spill . . .
        the streams mingling . . . the shaping basin . . .
            strata of heat and chill . . .

as being surges, swells through matter,
    riding out a vector . . .
        inertia quickens inert water
            with contour . . . this vague spectre

of green burgeoning . . . the flowing shape
    whirls particles and passes . . .
        name writ in water . . . speed incarnate . . .
            erasing as it races . . .

(or, at the seam of currents, biding,
    subduing with formal power,
        enduring as old tunes survive
            the singer of the hour) . . .

transient substance rotates through,
    and pattern gives . . . persists . . .
        as quatrains shrink and stretch and chew
            whatever verbal grist . . .

as thought rolls through experience
wave organizes sea . . .
   as soul contrives its turbulence
    from diet of entropy . . .

  fast fashioning its seething crest . . .
    tons churning through its core . . .
      wide arc and sharp . . . from the black past . . .
     now leaning toward the shore.

EVE: NIGHT THOUGHTS

okay so the wheel bit was a grinding bore
and fire a risk in the cave never mind the dogs
he brings home and cows and I can endure
his knocking rocks for sparks and rolling logs
it's his words that get on my nerves his incessant naming
of every bird or bug or plant his odd
smirk as he commits a syllable taming
Nature with categories as though the Word were God

okay so statements were bad enough
and accusations crossing spoiling digestion
but then he invented the laugh
next day he invented the question
I see it he's busy building a verbal fence
surrounding life and me but already I
counterplot I'll make a poem of his sense
by night as he dreams I am inventing the lie

EDEN REVISITED

Here is all humidity and committees,
   drunk to bed and solace of the groin.
I think of that thin air, free around old granite,
   detest myself--and often think of going . . . .

      Stepping out of the car onto dry pine needles
      I breathed it all back with the scent of age . . .
      boys with canvas packs and bare knees
      climbing, with the long breathing of prophets,
      sleeping slim and brown in celibate bedrolls,
      dreaming vines of flowering hypotheses
      by incense flickering in the spatial night.

      I remember purity of fright,
      of shivering, of laughter in the rain,
      of afternoon, the mystery of morning
      before the sun, and gladness of light,
      the ether chill of mountain water.

      Returning, fat and scant of breath, I saw
      peaks breaking clouds on their shoulders,
      sun-cured faces of granite, faces of leather,
      emitting aspen in year after year of weather . . . .

One may easily be readmitted, wearing
   his glands like sores, thoughts like snakes,
and climb and have a smoke upon the summit,
   descend, and camp with whiskey by the lakes.

But are those moral mountains not all fakes,
   a nursery of stuffed animals? Wishing

is indulgence, my evening Eve. Would you want
more than an hour's hike, a weekend's fishing?

Oh, I, too, feel the thickening of white flesh
and panic of the brink, and sliding, sliding--
but for all our tears for innocence, would we change
the guilt of doing for the guilt of hiding?

HELP! I AM A PRISONER IN A CHINESE COOKIE FACTORY

I sell. All sell something, but all say
selling one's soul or hole or art is crime.
What kind of woman do you think I am? I am.
What you pay me to say, I say. In rhyme? I rhyme.

A hack of a magic mirror, I give you back
your image as you dream you should appear.
You name it, Bud: I answer like an echo
and simulate submission, front or rear.

My heart is that fabled singer, Orifice,
who goes to Hell to save Your Idiocy.
My mind, a calculator, leaps to the touch
of buttons. Selfless, I sell--of self am free.

Yet my venality is all in vain:
I have not rooted out my deepest I--
for when the cookie crumbles, still there comes
(distant, anonymous) this comic cry.

TO MY RELUCTANT STUDENTS OF POETRY

My dog, house-broken, sleeping in the shade,
fattening, and petted past all lusting,
no longer sniffs at danger, no longer begs.
He will not starve. He dies there, well-adjusting.

My nervous father always had a goal,
devoting all his sense to beat the bank.
His end was practical--but all he left
was debt and memory of how he drank.

My mother, for security, sold twice
the quivering scarlet bushel of her heart.
One man threw darts at it. The other still
ignores it as it darkly flakes apart.

My wife could never honestly believe
in being what they trained her for from birth.
But having failed to be the bitch the world
rewards, she cannot now believe her worth.

And I have daughters tenderly aware
that life is to be lived. Their minds run loose.
Tomorrow they will don school uniforms
and learn to dedicate themselves to use.

Enlightenedly self-interested, my nation
dispenses cunningly, with kind contentment,
its wealth upon the water, but is hurt
by underdeveloped thanks and black resentment.

I am myself indifferent useful, knowing
the social forms and how to get ahead;
but if, at times, I wake to uselessness
and find delight in not yet being dead,

my numb soul stirs, as a dog will wake to bark,
disturbed by a deeply-layered jungle dream.
Involuntarily I shout the poem:
Perhaps we are more human than we seem.

TRANSLATED FROM THE SWAHILI

Swinging a torch in the black wind,
    alert for jungle eyes,
I do not hear my lady come
    on fur-hinged thighs.

My lady comes riding a tiger!
    Her breathing blisters lips!
I moan beside the gleaming river
    scorched by fingertips!

Drums pump all night the river.
    Dark star, white star, twinned.
I sweat in celebration, sweeping
    circles in the wind.

And in the dawn sun, bleeding,
    I wait return of night--
the rising wind, the blind drums,
    the tiger bite.

EPITHALAMIUM:

INTERLOCKING

(to be etched on a ring with the last line leading into the first)

looking outward
softly rocking
harbor ease
turning flocks
in ancient order
tipping take
the golden breeze
heeling starboard
wild the wake
taut the tackle
deep the keel
rooted blackly
churning sod
nervy tendrils
thorny stem
lifting aloft
the blossom wheel
the crusty pod
the thistledown
in autumn floating
maidenly

to earthy brown
breast as soft
as rib is white
interlocking
in the night
craftily
beneath the skin
tick-tocking
thieves delight
slice the tangle
sharkswift fin
arcing into
morning laughter
plums and cherries
popping ripe
languid limbs
sheets of sunshine
sudden stripe
the thought of after
rocking softly
turning inward

THE UNCHOSEN

I guess I have a deficiency. God never
said boo to me when as a boy I stood
straining in church with muscular endeavor
for the sweet squirt of salvation. I never could
see why He spoke to this or that old lady,

sending her, hallelujah, down the aisle.
Was I alone in the congregation vile?
Or was their claim of spirit something shady?
And now when I read poets who simply Know,
drinking their imagery from God's own cup,

whose poems "just come," and then, like Topsy, grow,
whereas I always have to make them up,
with never a tremor saying *Break this line*
or *Save this phrase, regardless of its beat,*
hear no obscurities which seem Divine,

and, knowing not God's measure, still count feet,
I yearn that reason give me some relief
(besides those lapses when my mind, not soul,
is not so much inspired as out of control).
Non-linear God, help Thou my unbelief!

WAITING AROUND FOR MOBY DICK

To me with my pole arched
above the brackish swill around the dock,
patient, patient as Indian wrestlers sitting
all night with a forearm lock,

he will not come, nor nibble
my minnow bait. Should I then cast loose
over vacant, heaving seas and bore the mist
of the North, or the South's slow sun?
Should I run mad, as the mad have always run?
Ah, ease of the muscles, flexing of the fist!
Dreaming a wild war, I am trapped in truce,
eroding in time's long dribble.

I read a book that promises defeat
even of Argosies supplied and skilled,
of subsequent misuse of golden fleece,
of Jasons, bluntly mortal, mocked and killed.
I read another saying that success
lay not in having done but in the doing,
that virtue makes its way to heavenly banks
and lies secure, with interest accruing,

and now am tense (too dark to read)
with springs compressed and ready rod,
waiting around in hope of going down
dead, silly, lashed to a sounding god.

ON MOUNTAIN FORK

discipline:
                the whispering *s* of line
above the canoe, the weightless fly thrown through
a gap in the branches, spitting to rest
on the still pool where the bass lay,
                                        wrist true
in the toss and flick of the skipping lure.

love:
        silence and singing reel, the whip
of rod, chill smell of fish in the morning air,
green river easing heavily under, drip
of dew in brown light.
                        At the stern I learned
to steer us--wavering paddle like a fin.

art:
        tyrannous glances, passionate strategy,
the hush of nature, humanity slipping in,
arc of the line, ineffectual gift
of a hand-tied bug, then snag in the gill, the snap
and steady pull.
                        His life was squalid, his

temper mean, his affection like a trap.
I paddled on aching knees and took the hook.
My father shaped the heart beneath my skin
with love's precision:
                        the gift of grief, the art
of casting clean, the zeal, the discipline.

COLLEGE, 1966

Dear folks,
Sorry I haven't written, but, you see,
I'm busy seeking my Identity.
I've hunted high and low. I prod and pinch,
examining my navel inch by inch.
So far no luck--and what to do about it?
I find I'm getting on quite well without it.
I'd get a new one--at whatever cost--
but I'd be out of style if I weren't lost.

Aside from that, my life is getting hipper.
I'm called "The Coffee Shop Relationshipper."
My peer group finds me an essential cog
in our eternal random dialogue.
Believe it, I am *in*--or out so far
I never think a thought that's linear.
My eyes are glazed--but, Mom, that's not from rumming.
I'm moving out of Being. I'm Becoming.

I got an A in Primary Regression
and gave myself a B in Self-Expression.
A C in Non-Productive Thought Creation
was due to lapses in my Meditation.
I did not qualify for Viet Nam:
The draft board cannot tell what sex I am.
I'm doing lots of push-ups in the Glen--
for Phiz Ed: That's called Isometric Zen.

Professor Peter Pan has now explained
that life as lived by you is mostly feigned.
Adults play games--but each weekend *we* go
into the woods to exercise our Ego.
In non-directive groups we all are free

to train ourselves in Sensitivity,
which means we pick each other all apart,
demolishing defenses with good heart,
exposing all the ugly things we think
and begging to be loved although we stink.

How false your life of work and business dealings!
We've learned there is no Truth except our Feelings.
No goal is worth the effort, lest it be
saving allowance for some LSD.
(How clear it is that things seem what they're not
when one is launched into the Truth by pot!)
I wish you folks could take a little T
and learn to appreciate your darling,

                                        Me.

IN THE FACULTY LOUNGE

I hover by the box marked mine as pale
as a lover waiting his fair dame's abuse,
watching the manicured fingers sort the mail

till I may dangle in my daily news.
A list of books I cannot buy nor read.
A device to solve my problems, once it's mastered.

Rejections right and left. An ad for seed.
A reader writes to tell me I'm a bastard.
Colleagues are sweeping past me like race horses.

My family regrets I turned out rotten.
My friends are getting ulcers or divorces.
PAST DUE are bills for goods I have forgotten.

Remember that young poet whom I failed?
I see that he just won a Pulitzer Prize.
Another, whom I passed, has just been jailed

and needs a reference, graduateschoolwise.
A committee to eliminate committees
wants me to chair a meeting all day Sunday.

Foundation heads from all the Eastern cities
will drop in for a chat at dawn on Monday.
Just think how here and there across the nation,

across the campus, even across the seas,
people address to me such flagellation!
I pant beside the mailbox on my knees.

THE VISITATION

These January trees are frozen ganglia,
rigid nerves upturned under the powdery sky,

and I face glass, press flesh to cold, my back
to the warm room full of Philharmonic. I turn

to ponder the red fire. These books, these pictures,
this tireless lamp . . . .
                                    Is death so absolute?

Through death--the random snow, the startled trees.
Grieving again, I lean to the chilled pane.

The yard is in the room, in me the wasted
leaves, the grey patches, the dormant branches,

and you are here, are here. Signals in air,
the feeding current, the whispering gas, the vein

of light that spills upon my table. This love
that tints the page, between the poem and myself,

this urgency to say it well, this relish
of the world as it flakes and fades . . .
                                    it must be you.

ELEGY FOR A PROFESSOR OF MILTON
(for Albert Liddle, 1896-1967)

I cannot say once more ye laurels, nor
summon from shaded eyes a melodious tear.
The elegance that with your passing passed
demands diapsons, but we cannot hear
today the organ tones of eloquence.

Like sophomores who nodded in your class,
unequal to the challenges you posed,
we face the luminous with darkened glass
and slump before the dignity of truth.
And yet into our inarticulate trance

comes echoing your majestic utterance: death.
The toughened young demanding relevance
discern a distant trumpet sounded by
some straggler on the torn, relinquished field
and wonder at the loyalty of one

who, in some forgotten battle, will not yield.
What was the cause? Something about Milton?
Something about how that young man refused
to tolerate life--or death--devoid of meaning?
Some fury that some talents are misused?

Some faith that in a free and open encounter
rightness would prosper, error be exposed,
the venal could be driven from the Temple
(where they, God knows, for ages have reposed)?
And, now, have we heard the last notes from

a trumpet which survived the bomb's eclipse?
Did one out there in the mist-hung battleground
form noble music with his dying lips?
Has that historic war, we rightly question,
anything much to do with here and now?

Dear friend, professor, who lived what you professed,
you would not, if you heard these words, allow
a claim to glory or a spur to grief.
Were I to call you hero you would smile.
Wryly humble, you force me to be honest:

That distant trumpet was not quite your style.
But, Albert, grant me, when a shepherd drowns,
another somewhat loudly sweeps the string.
Your way of life was music in the dark--
I say to one who knew himself to sing.

AT THE DANCING SCHOOL OF
THE SISTERS SCHWARZ

Silently grave as voyeurs in a powder room,
we fathers sit with coats folded on knees
this visiting day, watching Miss Hermene
teach fourteen girls the elements of ballet.

Accompaniment is struck in chords upon
the Steinway grand. Outside a siren grieves:
law for a speeder below. Miss Hermene slaps
time on her thighs, her words exact and low.

Her muscular, liquid arms demonstrate grace
to daughters in pink tights along the bar.
Battement tendu! and fourteen arches curve.
She spots a limp leg, squats for a better view,

then sweeps from child to child, chin high, commanding--
love in her old eyes, discipline on her tongue,
correct as a queen, and fierce beneath her charm.
Our girls come hushed and quick, hair back, nails clean;

chubby or bony, concave or convex of chest,
gangly, petite or tough, their slippers whisper
in the studio. No scratching or wriggling now,
but each projects life to her pointed toe.

My own, the smallest, still sticks out her tummy,
curving her limber spine. Her feet are flat,
her limbs thin. Braids swing as she takes correction
like kisses--with freckly cheeks and toothy grin.

Material comes raw, but Miss Hermene
makes girlflesh pirouette and count strict time.
Covertly I squirm--loosely sitting, like nature,
thinking how daffodils look to a worm.

Glissez! Sautez! Pliez! Knees skinned at skating
now bend in diamond shapes around the room,
and fathers dream of the stage where ballerinas
are purer than people, selfless, without age,

and Miss Hermene in her Ohio winter
dreams rigorous designs for the new day
and tender swarm: the power of grace, the truth
of timing, the immortality of form.

THE DAY OF THE FIRE DEPARTMENT'S FIFTIETH ANNIVERSARY PARADE

Across the rasping row of cars from years
when you and I were children I saw your face
brown as September, firm as solid pears,
searching a space in that slow honking race.
You came, with chin aloft, while men in blue
rattled their drums, shifted flags, marked time.
You joined the kids on the curb. We straggly few
watched the parade subside to pantomime--
and then resume, a marching band, the trucks,
red, gold, with hoses, pumps, deliberate choir
howling their turtle progress, grinding flux
of noise announcing that there was no fire.
I watch you laugh. The majorette's a bore.
And when there is no fire, I love you more.

HARD

listen it's not only the Viet Cong but these
long-haired kids on BMW's naked at night
hauling off my substance like a train of ants
through jungles flakes of flesh in their mandibles
to roll it and smoke it somewhere out of sight

and these upstart bucks spreading violence
like popping pustules all over my USA
staring me down like my own daughter pregnant
with insolence cool you know like France
after all we've done for her acting that way

when all Washington knows how to do is raise
taxes appoint a half-assed committee picks
some pipsqueak general to run Asia plays
007 with its Dogberry CIA you can't tell me
somebody isn't behind these foreign flicks

what we need is action castrate the Arabs
and wire 10 million volts into all these
electric guitars fry their beards send these mobs
to cotton patches in outer Idaho
and give SNCC back to the Chinese

it's all right there in LIFE spread out in full
color conspirators from Havana meeting
in sheets burning draftcards to light their joints
you think the streets are safe? you think you'll
collect the rent each month and escape a beating?

me I'm taking more pills and enjoying them less
my wife looking gaunt dangerous antsy
my yard has gone to pot my kids dropped out
and you think just one thermonuclear device
in the right place would be you say chancy?

CHROMATIC

Owing to drugs or astronomic explosions
all colors were confused.
                              I knew when I
woke on sahara sheets and gazed, alas,
at violet wifeflesh sleeping like a distant range.

Beyond her, orange slats across the sky--
pale green in the June morning. Black the grass
and utter white the boughs with their black leaves.
In the yard my mauve feet cool in the black dew.

News
        on the pink screen
                              explained nothing. Strange,
that whole long day rotating in changing light,
and stranger still the rioting scarlet negroes
exploding like summer all the scarlet night.

THOSE SHEETS OF FIRE

These hot nights are broken
by soundless puffs of light

and, after gasps of time,
that disconnected rumbling.

(Each morning the news shows
walls have buckled, windows

are starry shards. We hear
air torn by sirens, the thud

of dark flesh, the sharp
information of shots, see

the hard lips under helmets.)
Hate squats on the heart

of the far city. Here we
kiss and kiss, after

each soft flash clinging,
counting, certain that sound

comes blackly on, at least
a thousand feet per second.

EVIDENCE FOR THE DOCTRINE OF A SEPARATE CREATION

                    alone
              among the animals
                 man kills
           his kind he has designs
              mortality fills
      his mind no velvet leopard ever
              died for justice
               slew with love
              nor is his prey
         politically assassinated
                   they
                (the beasts)
        are not inclined to suicide

                 orangutans
           in cages sometimes may
                 jerk half
         their adolescent hours away
             and maybe a rare
                chimpanzee
                  is gay
      man's friend the dog will mount
             a leg or bitch
          line up to take his turn
            and not care which
                but man
                  alone
         goes rutting all the year
         preferring almost any
               to his mate
          devising means to be
               infertile
                spraying

his seed like shells
laying to be laying it
takes a man
to copulate
in hate
he plugs up any orifice around
or finding none
will fertilize the ground

only
a man
would sew up skins to hide
his loins and decorate himself
in pride
or shame
tattoo scars on his flesh or wear
a badge to indicate his rank
slaves labor
deep in African earth
to deck blonde hair
with diamonds
whales are drained of ambergris
so that milady may outsmell her neighbor
no other species
has the need to find
some drug or drink to free
it from
its mind
beasts never go to war to fight for peace

man
measures time
gives names
he shapes the stone

```
          aware of his own death
            therefore at odds
               with nature
       he torments himself with gods
                 erect
            among the animals
                 alone
```

THE HITLER IN OUR HEARTS

Reading all the grand old poems of war
resistance, my blood burns. I feel renewed--
cleaning and oiling my manhood, snapping my hammer.
I think of one bombed baby and grow lewd
with brotherhood, something worth fighting for.
O Dove of Peace on my banner, I could not love
thee half so much loved I not honor more.

Justice shall overcome, our tattered bands
storming the Winter Palace of Evil, hurling
flowers and non-negotiable demands . . .
I dream, snarling at wife and kids when they
cling to me, wanting security and such.
Hush darlings. If it weren't for Daddy's honor
he swears he could not love ye half so much.

A DECADE OF AMERICAN POETRY: 1957-67

No question: we were too genteel, if that's
the word for mentalities which gave
that '49 award to Pound, retreating
from human value, disregarding meaning.
Only professors could defend a point
by swallowing erudite ugliness--or those
Quartets without music--nor joy nor love nor light,
but lots of certitude. As C. P. Snow
told us, the literary mind at best
was irresponsible, at worst pernicious,
most charming when most innocently effete.

Ten years ago our poets were coming back
from Fulbrights bearing sheafs of landscape poems
with colons in their titles, mincing, rare:
"Penzance: Bank Holiday," or "Twilight: Villa
de los Huesos Secos." Everyone was writing
poems about Bruegel. Rago was weary
of historical monologues about the Duchess
of Portsmouth explaining Original Sin to Rowley.
The Fisher King, like Mistah Kurtz, was dead.
Tiresias was a scholar. Jarrell pondered
fertility embodied in a girl
who dozed in a library. We all were dozing
in libraries. Fertility flipped out
to demonstrate at lunch counters. Ciardi--
having assaulted Mrs. Lindbergh--said
the most probable word in *Poetry* was *improbable*,
"the improbable rose," "her improbable smile," that faint
bemused, impersonal irony we all
relished in our refinement. When Ginsberg
said poetry in *Hudson* in the fifties
was simply unreadable, he was dead right.

In the New York *Times* a buoyant Lowell hailed
the West Coast Renaissance, and promptly abandoned
pentameter and classical allusions,
began to sell fillets of tattered heart.
(Who touches his *Life Studies* touches a man.)
Somewhere were dug up Patchen and Rexroth, who
come out for revolutions like the green
of St. Patrick's. Poets read to jazz (remember
jazz?), stripped, smoked pot as Dad smoked cornsilk, cursed.
(Heroin was exotic--for musicians.)
Books were promoted by censorship and raids
while picture-spreads in *LIFE* at long last brought
poetry to the attention of commuters.
How innocent and distant seem those days
when refugees from Black Mountain were ranging
from Majorca to Albuquerque, sitting at
the feet of guru Rexroth in the West,
the feet of guru Williams in the East--
Levertov, Olson, Creeley, Blackburn, Goodman--
with lines of nervous breath, images of
profound simplicity. When Pound was freed--
that guru of White Citizens' Councils--he
removed the fascist stain from Whitman's vision.
Negro became the *lingua franca*. Values
reversed, as in a photo negative
where hot looks cool: achievement, wealth, success
were black (or, rather, white). One scoured for junk
to cherish: poverty, pain, and slovenly dress,
sexual aberration, drugs, whatever
elders considered vulgar or obscene.
The blacks were used (why did they not resent it?)
as guides to degradation, as connections
to the cool world of grass and rock-and-roll.
This conscious search for sin was clearly also
a search for innocence, for sexlessness,

Shapiro, back before he proclaimed himself
the Peck's Bad Boy of the Establishment,
said if he had one book on a desert island
he'd want the poems of Lawrence, that bristly daddy
of all the angry outs to ask for blood.
Shapiro talked of starting a magazine--
but not some little secretive emission
tolerated by friends. He wanted a *LIFE*
with pictures, color, sex--and circulation.
Was poetry an escape from emotion, or
a catalyst which occurred at the intersection
of Brooks and Warren? Ogden and Richards? Did
Hayakawa class it with advertising?
Let poetry burst through the bric-a-brac
and wave its stubby selfhood in the face
of the Committee on Explication. McCarthy
died, 1957, while *Howl* was heard
as a depraved moan in the ruins. Ciardi saw it
while slouched on my couch with Dant in hand. I'd called
it unreadable--but Ciardi did not sneer.
He quoted, "in the total animal soup of time,"
and there pronounced, "If Whitman is poetry,
then that is poetry." (In those lost days
one quarreled whether things were poetry.)
But even he sought jewels in the lava flow.
That's how we all were taught to read--for phrases,
symbols, for art, at least for pattern, wit--
but if these qualities occurred at all
in the new torrent, they were rubble of
museums. You don't sit by and watch the madman
shaking his dead geranium in your face
and analyze his language. The tide was sweat--
and in it many drowned. Some learned to swim.

for endless puberty, release from mind,
a refusal to mature in the Western World,
a yearning for an Eastern sweet unreason . . . .

And how this product sold! For in a guilty
nation, nothing succeeds like defeat. Grove Press
and *Playboy* made it plain there's money in
rebellion. Corso sold like Evtushenko.
Ferlinghetti sold like Ogden Nash.
(And New Directions seemed as staid as Knopf.)
Avant and pop were suddenly all the same!
Elvis, James Dean and Marilyn Monroe
made it in to be out. (Intellectual pets,
these shaggy fairy rock groups.) In ten years
mass media, once object of aversion,
became the great white hope in blinking lights
for the hipcult. Riesman predicted all:
McLuhan made it cool to be what we
are bound to become--other-directed, tribal.
And inarticulate poetry is at least
democratic. Anyone can do it. All
can understand. Ignorance is a kind
of primitive virtue. Poetry, which once
was too cerebral, now was oral (on
its way to becoming genital), and poets thrived
on records, in college readings, entertaining
at parties of the rich--the new jongleurs.

And all the publishing professors perished,
in word and influence if not in deed.
Wilbur's prophet cried in the wilderness.
Nemerov, Roethke, Kunitz, Simpson, Jarrell--
writing as much as ever, and as well,
gained something from the popularity
of poetry in general, but sensed they were
outmoded. Many began translating. They

wrote about Goya now--and race, and war--
attempted to limber up their lines, to find
a narrative mode, dramatic mode. Some followed
Lowell to booths of confession; some followed Bly
to fish in the deep snow for images
which might unlock their hopelessly rational minds.
We looked to Snodgrass to teach us about how
to emerge from the self's swamp to social comment,
retaining the mind's music, a sense of shape,
and saw skill grow while his ambition faltered.
Dickey put on a good show, telling tales
of making a girl in an abandoned car,
a stewardess falling out of an airplane, or
the plight of sunburned lovers--a poet with
competence and no mission--like so many.
And older men wrote on: MacLeish and Frost,
Auden and Cummings. *J.B.* cried out the fate
of virtue, quality, in a world obsessed
with boils--a lean form speaking to the times,
his impact lost in the hurly-burly tide.
Auden was launching one book after another
with reason's keel and irony's tricky rudder,
archaic as justice--and as unexciting.
Alas that wit in Auden as in Adlai
was such a pinpoint, though affirming, flame.
When Cummings died the hippies took no notice
of that bohemian dinosaur. Frost died,
dismissed by Lowell as a "great pre-modern,"
though he alone of modern poets took
true cognizance of current science and thought.
And Williams toppled, that other snowy giant,
as left of Frost as Yeats and Eliot
had been to his right--and no howl that I heard
bemoaned his passing. (Remember the elegies
for Dylan? Thomas, I mean.) I heard Ginsberg

explain to a college crowd why Williams failed
to measure up to the highest poetic standards:
"He never got laid enough," sad Allen said.
And who has sung for Eliot, who seemed
himself to have forgotten how to sing?

No question. The impulse of the decade was right:
to find a new engagement, an audience,
to find a cause, protest forms which held nothing,
to be human again--itchy of crotch and barefoot.
It even seemed a noble undertaking
to find a substitute for alcohol.
But what did we discover? All roads led
to that delicious word, laving us softly:
self, self, self, self, self, self, and again self.
How we prefer personalities to products,
poets to poems--not art, but the private man!
Commitment? To Love? To love of being flaccid--
for who needs poetry who can have acid?
To freedom? The passive freedom of the trance,
each one engaged in onanistic dance.
Negroes be damned: the demonstration's over,
Mother is properly shocked, the pot delivered.
If peace can be achieved by turning on
(or off, or out), why organize resistance?
And social justice, like art, requires an effort.
The only relevance is here and now
and you and me, and sometimes I wonder whether
you are as relevant as once you seemed.
The strobe lights flash, the music screams *we're free,*
Ginsberg redcords each Texaco marquee . . .
Is this the revolution of which we dreamed?

Beneath the din the voice of reason drones
untiring with its necessary labor.

Depend on the professors to survive.
Hardly a campus now without its poet--
a tweedy type, articulate at meetings,
a station-wagon, kids, a pretty wife,
insistent on his raises, gives good readings,
has half a heart for poetry, half for life.
By night he sharpens weapons. He learns, he learns.
You got to believe his heart in silence burns.
His anger builds, his focus narrows, his tools
lie ready in bright array. There'll come a day,
after the last great Happening, when he
will clear his throat and stand--with something to say.

RUMORS OF CHANGE: 1968-1978

Battle of Chicago

You are a member. (This message scrambles when
grey people try to read it.) You are a member
(you intersection in the network, capsule
in the streams of change).
                  We are the agents locking
eyes a silent instant, moving on.
It is important we know we belong.
                     What happened
in Chicago (while we heaved together many-
headed, linked by limbs and chained in spirit,
spreading--inside, outside the hall, across
the pulsing night into homes where we gathered and wept,
the nodules warm and moist, the fibres tingling)
I say what happened in Chicago was
we co-opted the media. Newsmen now are of
our number. Never can the grey ways go
unknown nor can we fail to recognize
ourselves in halls of mirrors. Did you not catch
those locking eyes from man to man, to you
right through the screen? They said we know, we know . . . .

(1) Words are not fast enough: We must rely
on rumors in recesses of the brain,
as, now, saying this, I am seized by tremors
of strength and joy, love in the air, knowledge
that you are there, infusing my fingers, electric.
You are writing word-by-word this message.

(2) We must form groups of twelve to meet on Thursdays
at eight in one another's homes. Drop all
conflicting commitments. Form groups. Form is necessary now. (Formality and form-
lessness become the grey, the grey become

formal and formless.) Form environments
of change, of force and reinforcement. Let
there be light

                refreshments and no set agenda.

(3) These rumors must be spread in chain mail. We
have access to means of reproduction. Glut
the air with rumors, nominate all who
will understand and send them all. Our code
is unbreakable. Like DNA we have
neither authority nor copyright.

(4) Stay on the cutting edge of indirection--
as the surfer upright on his wave, the skier
slicing right and left the unforgiving
slope, the sailor tacking tight and close,
the diver having left the board. Remember
not to remember. The river never rests.
(Guilt is self-indulgence; there is no time
for explanation, argument, no time
to bicker, as the bead of attention burns
through onrushing years.) Our plight is dire and our
direction shifting swiftly. We move in gladness,
committed, tacking, knowing speed on the edge
of failure, knowing never to take the slope
head-on, to flap in irons, the tiller loose,
the bow in a cone of wind.

                Review: There is
just time for this review. The name of our
network is change, we publish these rumors, we
celebrate our membership on fixed
occasions, we keep in touch by means of surges
of feeling crossing the earth like prayer.

                            (Did I
say we accept conversions? We accept conversions,
knowing a grey one shows his kingliness

as simply as one turns a card: it is all
there--the grey back, the scarlet face and sceptre,
awaiting and giving benediction. We
are bound to each by the Hitler in our hearts
and our grey sides turned under.)
                                    We circulate
rumors to every member we know. (I say
this in a poem so that you can be sure
I mean it literally.)
                            You have received.
We are, eyes locked, in touch. It is now your move.
Our move

And a Silver Rose for HHH

Your signals, be assured, are coming in:
the web shudders with their breath
                                and the dew falls.
I walk in the morning with a straight back, wearing
your radiance, authorized by our membership
to promote and be promoted. We have all
attained the highest rank and are still ascending.

On cathedral steps in Barcelona--prizes
for poems in Catalan: third prize, a silver
rose; second prize, a golden rose; first prize,
of course, a real rose. We have surely learned
freedom from envy of the golden rose.)

News of the week:
                        Everywhere oughts are dis-
appearing, as shadows absorbed by flowers when
the sun climbs. Everywhere I see oughts shrink
in spreading light. Science removes them as
carbon tet removes a greasy stain.
Muscles regain their juice and joints work freely,
spirit coheres with flesh when oughts are shed.

The camera judges not.
The revolution
clearly is based on fact--not riot but
discovery, not war but truth surging
in the main.
Their candidate has a face crosshatched
with shadows. He will win the golden rose
while the real
cocks its head at ought
in utter
incomprehension, dies, and recurs, recurs . . .
even in this our garden,
Kingdom of Midas.
(Thank you for sharing with me this, your poem.)

Close Encounters of the New Left Kind

They will not be persuaded. Every word
has an equal and opposite reaction. (No
words but these--the whispering of members.)
They have small means for responding to seduction.
Imperatives are futile, such as
Change!
or *Learn!* or *Love!*
As agents we are secret
architects--or farmers. Godly we parcel
the void with impersonal walls, clearing the gardens
where nature can occur. Change structure and
their attitudes will change.
Should we not set
a good example? Build propitious forms?
And may we not walk naked, you and I,
in our electric mist of squirming light?
(Ah, how their shoulders would unslope, their mouths
untwist, voices unwhine, their eyes grow soft
and steady--seeing how we must feel, being us!)

Rather--expect the assassin's crosshair aim.
I heard one mutter in soliloquy,
"He hath a dayly beauty in his life
that makes me ugly."--*Iago*.

                  Backlash is
a physical phenomenon, and our
realm is the real. No, let us not walk there
glowing, but take our skin, hot from the day's
labor, home to a sound sleep, and then
perhaps on harvest evenings we may lean
on the fence by the full field, silhouetted
in the bulging sun, sucking a spear of wheat.

Election Night: 1968

Again O Ancyent Marinere you grip
me with skinny hand, accuse me of having lost
a day
        an hour
              while minds lock, tumblers click/
click, then the silence, leaving a hairline crack,
decision made, a nation undecided.
Already voters' eyes look like ballbearings.

Time is necessity, and there is time
for the necessary. I hear you, membership.
The surf of your voices is an aggregate
of whispers hinting: The Ptolemaic system
cannot be broken from within. Hinting:
aesthetics = ethics = science.
Hinting: Psyche is random energy;
spirit is psyche with intent, as wired
to the source and turning on itself producing
light. (I take each whisper of surf and spread
it instantly upon the wind.) I am

the Ancyent Marinere in the mirror, telling
myself beware: the cone of wind

                              (abstractions

can put a poem in irons). Beware: the golden
rose

      ("Politics is of the machine age, ob-
solete."--*B. Fuller*).
                          O Ancyent Marinere
(inhabitant of every poem, every
revolution) we know urgency lifts us
beyond panic. When we know the wire is going
dead in seconds, each syllable must count:
aesthetics = ethics = science

                              over/

                                out

Regrouping

Last Thursday when we launched the revolution
it lifted like a rocket from the pad
and then subsided. We are in irons. We know
so little about how it feels to move, to fly.
Bound in this chrysalis our energy swells,
impulses storm, we ache, unsure if what
is on our backs

                    might not be wings. O worm,
what larva can design a butterfly?

My child is screaming in the night. She is
braindamaged. And from the coils of sleep I stagger
to her cage. On knees I reach through cold bars, grip
that squalling mouth with fury, oh furious love.
After the fight she knows to let it come--
the love, the discipline. When I relax
my hand she holds it there, wanting it wanting
it hard across her mouth a minute more.

Instructively cruel I pull away, pad creaking
into silent dark.
                    Let it come, my grip is loving.
You and I are braindamaged, needing
release of flight, swathed as a mummy, screaming
with aimless strength, banging the empty drawers
in our house of mind.
                    For C-groups (for Change, for Chrys-
alis). We are a Movement, not an Or-
ganization. C-ers, let these signals through
the jamming.
                    Ease in my grip.
                              My voice is you.

From Communion to Community

Is this a joke, you ask, is this a meeting
or a party?
                    Seeking action or escape?
And should we, hearing history's thunderous question,
form a committee?
                    Organization?
                              Should we
few who are free now greyly organize?
I say
        organ
            ize, eyes, I's
                        (have it!)
                              Vote
as organs vote: The politic body moves
fluently singing, a chorus of minute voices,
each crying clearly *Me! Me!* The stone upon
the Western World is condemnation of self,
the radical the one who can admit

sense of oppression.
                    The selfish cell divides,
generous with its nucleus, its membrane
semipermeable, parting like skin
of a bubble. "Our unity is that of the flame,
not of the stone."--*N. Weiner*. The center has no
fixed shape nor size, the limits hazy: thus
the units, protean, repeating, and alive.

I yawn, stretch, spreading the wealth, receiving
news,
          myself an intricate democracy.
Tell me exactly what you mean.
                              I mean
you cannot sail directly into the wind.
I mean "Rumor = ambiguity x importance."
--*G. Allport*. Midas, I mean, died hungry, such
is the golden lure of definition. I mean
we are not thing nor shape but process, not
water of wave but energy/ pattern/ shape--
our thingness stepping from the wave as Venus
expressed the essence of the sea. I mean
death is our reason for living, and this strange joy
is phosphorescence of decay. I mean
(after Chicago) we would be fools to think
we could alter events. We would be fools to think
there is no hope.
                    Discover ease in fact.
(Paradox is the maze I keep my mouse in.)
Exactly what I mean is words
                              are/ snap/
shots/ of/ motion/ in/ many/ dimensions.
                                        Life
is at least a movie/ smelly/ feelie,
and our love flowers in a garden with
strong and invisible, utterly mobile, walls.

May Day May

Pitched on this sea, expansive canvas straining,
rigging taut over laboring tonnage of hull,
bulging current breaking like bombs at the bow,
empty air pouring its power upon us, who
are we?
                    (riding this weight in violent weather)
but a whisper of intelligence at the tiller,
our quarter-inch of leverage telling whether
we head up into failure
                              or fall off,
leaning the fast and easy way to waste.

With talon grip you tell me, Ancyent Marinere,
it is too late, we are not at the tiller.
We are prostrate on the deck, awash in the flow
of the scuppers:
                    That is a spectre looming at
the helm with eyes like cones of fire. I ask:
Who are we but spectres of spectres, agents
of spirit? We have seized control of all
the psychic centers, are plugged in each to each,
participating in all the wireless wordless
messages of light.
                    Rebels have always captured
radio stations, the telephone exchange.
In the first black hour before a stone is pried
from the dawn street, one hears a shuffle of mimeograph machines in cellars discreetly curtained.
(Not propaganda. Information. The network
hums with the news.)
                    Our nation paves one million
acres per year *STOP* like a tin shed *STOP*
expanding economy *STOP* like a one-way lung
STOP circulation *STOP* persists only
in drainage *STOP*

We gather on Thursdays at eight.
Such facts catch in our tinder. Blow. Organize, let us gather at the synapses.
In the world's very nervous system let
us whisper
our glow

Middle Ages

Brethren, sistren, are we out of touch?
Rarely do barefoot members of our order,
begging and preaching, village to village, come
bearing communication. Saints are silent.
The media have lost interest. Prophets no
longer bother to cry doom.
Are you
listening? I think you are there. Perhaps
you are not there. More likely, snug in your
monastic nook, you labor over looms
for the tourist market.
Here we are watching stars.
Fewer and fewer flying objects are
unidentified. For several years
running I forgot to renew my membership.
Last fall no one harvested hemp before
the frost, things got that bad.
Dark ages last
a thousand years. Scratching my hairy belly
through my robe, my feet before the fire,
I think there still is time, I think there will
always be time, always this now, always
this mote of urgency in the eye of God.
Messiahs trouble my dreams. I hope no more
messiahs come to save the world. The world

can only save itself--the cleansing fire,
fern growing fast on the charred land of spring--
if we will let it.   Now the winter sun
slices the slot of my carrel only a few
hours each afternoon, illuminating
old books, the practices which should be saved--
formulae, ceremonies, facts.   Surely
these will be needed once the plague has passed,
the boundaries rearranged.
                    We were the cut-
ting edge, at every crossroads wild revivals
with eucharist of acid.   That was no life
for children.
             Now in our scattered communes in
the crags we keep households where kids may grow
outside the law.   I cannot keep those brawling
nations straight.   There is only one weapon
against the state: indifference.
                          Stay in touch
and I will keep the record.   Signed, your scribe.

From Community to Communication

Love equals people times the square of the speed
of light.
         If we but knew the way to split
our atoms of isolation, paradise
might be regained.   Pipes are frozen under
the slow snow now.   We sleep together mostly
to save our scanty firewood.   Maybe need
will mother love's invention.
                        Doing without
is how we learn to do.   The blizzard brings

neighbors together laughing at the store
as tumid pewter clouds let fall the seeds
of oblivion and renewal.
                        Should any find
these tattered words in the mud of the spring thaw,
carried by the spring flood, caught on the twigs
innocently greening, know words
                        came between
us, words tasted of apple, words blurred our vision,
built our empire, spread our cancer, words
troubled our sleep like sand, know words,
the curse of Babel, made the many out
of one, yet secretly as tendrils in
the soil these whispered affirmations still
convey the spirit back to one again.
Signed, one
            (lost under snow) who found words husked
of his name could winter well and bear the light.

After the Cleansing Fire

After the fire, a green burgeoning. After
scarlet excoriation, after blackened ruins,
rampant the running vines and the rank grass.
Surfeit of blossoms, the stout trunks thrusting.
Rodents explore. Birds circle and settle. Beetles
forage in new shade.
                        Water that was steam
patters the leaves, scours the boulders. Ash
works soggily into encrusted soil.

After the flood, the olive twig. After
empire a barbarous farmer dents his plow
on a buried cornice. The wanderer muses
in the green land, perched on a broken wall.
After the tempest a butterfly tips and wavers

in the still air.
                Flames sheet the crackling pines
and lava spreads its wide tongue on the mountain.
The city unloads its poison.
                                Dig in dig in.
The chemicals are in the earth, the spirit
surges in loins, and the dim sun glows like love
behind the smoke,
                silent in the ripping wind.

Bronowski Reconsidered

humanis minimalis: This skull is all
remaining of what once was a species spread
in deathgrip round the globe. No insect nor
microbe ever attained such range.
                                These creatures,
like certain forms of cancer, could convert
environments to their uses and construct
their habitations even in outer space.
Such rudimentary forms of intelligence
apparently lack the faculty to know
their own connection with the scheme of things--
as though programmed to kill the host, as though
oblivious to larger good, like moles
that tunnel behind their noses unaware.

Their *civilization* as they called it spread
as acid effervesces, spilled on stone,
each bubble forming, bursting, new ones rising,
none lasting more than a hundred years or so,
yet each one hailed as a trend.
                                You would be amused
to study histories, their prophets, their
designers, each claiming to know the key,
each looking round that bubble architecture

dreaming stability.

They had a craving
for death, monotony; so isolated
each from each, they thought life was a torment,
death an end.

They each had a name.

Just think
of individual names for all those billions,
each striving to assert somehow that name,
to shore against the end, as though the point
were to endure selfhood, leave a mark.

They left their marks.

It took us centuries
to dismantle their massive concentrations, scabs
of concrete crusted, smothering life.

We think
the ecological function of disease
must be to clear the way for change.

Of course
this skull and all the misery it contained,
though not benign, proved biodegradable.

The Therapeutic State

Doctor, I hear voices.

Tell me what
they seem to say.

Doctor, this is real.
Tell me how it seems.

I dream of tunnels,
walls of petal. Doctor, I am wading
in feathers.

What kind of feathers?

Black, and the air

is music.
        What kind of music?
                    Whale.
                            You think
that you hear whales?
                 Not hear so much as feel
blunt throbbing of penetration, hemispheres
of brain knitting along their edges, glow
of lava, squeal of glacial scrape, the sear
of stars, the salt of flesh. Just listen, Doctor,
how rootlets munch the minerals in your veins.

And do you often have these dreams?
                           Doctor,
I never wake, I only dream of waking.
And you are a disappearing smile in the air.
I can no longer hear, no longer read
the lines on your diploma. You are me,
absorbed like sunlight in my balmy cure.

No Way to Run a Railroad
      --Annie Dillard

Egoist, bloom, spreading your peacock plume.
Drench with your breath this thin and chill spring air.
Drunk on the liquor of earth, drug-drenched by sun,
sucking old snow, you open your petals like thighs,
exposing your tender pistil.
                      O soft explosion,
you invade my senses like sleep.
                      Your prodigal scarlet
is squandered on the fumbling bee, your bounty
could choke these acres with flowers, your roots could snarl
life from the loam with their infinite hairy extension.

Too much, too much.

> Nature does nothing by halves--
for every egg a million willing sperm
swarming the walls like bolsheviks, driven
by need, drowning all need in waste.

> > O God,
is this a sound economy? Is this
logical? Just? Has providence no sense
of careful planning? Fear of blind excess?
O drouth, O flood, O storm, O scorching sky!

So bombed by blooms blooms blooms,

> > why then am I
so held in check, so cursed by body juices,
calculating, counting, regulating,
mounting my life

> > to ride with so tight a rein?

O bloom, most selfish when most generous,
most joined when most apart,

> > why do I measure
my ebb and flow? Why close these valves? Why send
this hardhat down to engineer my heart?

Huck Drops Out

goodbye sir says i

> *i won't let no runaway*
niggers get by me if i can help it

> > *they*
went off and i got aboard the raft with jim
feeling bad and low

> *Drifting away downstream,*
dimming like memory of childhood under
the blinking eyes of towns on shore,

> > *i knowed*

very well i had done wrong i see it warn't
no use for me to try to learn to do
right

Huck, born wrong,

a body that don't get started
right when he's little ain't got no show

the cry
of treefrogs, splash of muskrats, songs of slaves
at dusk along the veins of the continent
drifting like outlaw dreams,

like seeping love,
then i thought a minute says to myself hold on
spose you'd a done right, give him up, would you
felt better then than what you're feeling now?
why no says i

i'd feel as bad

well then
says i so what's the use you learning to
do right when to do right is troublesome
and it ain't no trouble to do wrong and wages
is just the same?

i was stuck i reckoned i
wouldn't bother no more about it but after this
always do whichever come handiest at the time

like treefrogs, niggers, dreams,

like leaking love.

Our Rumors Now Are Ended

I feed the pigs--Pigena with her stiff
ears and Swinella, floppy, coy, or calculating, standing back while her sister
nudges the bucket, spilling the slop on her head.
"Life will do anything for a living."--*J. Ciardi*.

For her bad manners Pigena will go first
to slaughter. I ponder which is better
programmed to survive. They are so white
and fat.
         I watch the evening news. Their collars
are all too tight. The Mayor of Altoona
oinks treble with indignation after a Council
meeting. The girl who holds the microphone
doubles as Weatherlady. She has a twang
not all the speech courses at State College
could undo. Bold Bella nudged the bucket
once too often. The Shah is nudging the bucket.
They are all so barbered.
         I hear few rumors now,
and change is loose in my pocket, random, or
like gradual frost line reaching down, two feet,
three, four, seeking our deep pipes. I have
grave doubts I ever spoke for any members.
I haul wood mornings, ashes evenings, teach
kids fix cars feed pigs play bridge watch news.
"A low dishonest decade."--*W. H. Auden*.
Full of our clever hopes and heady dreams,
so outraged were we by the Gulf of Tonkin,
we had no outrage left for Creep and Crook,
the blind machinery of power bull-
dozing indifferently. I feed the pigs.
I pay their taxes, ride their highways, eat
their bacon. My IBM Selectric sips
their blood. I share the Mayor's grief:
Surely we need a better County Jail.
Ten years have made me younger, candid, grey,
and brought my dizzy arias down to scale.

"Our actors melted into air, thin air."
--*W. Shakespeare*. Our revels ended, where
art thou now, Charlie Reich? Where is thy Greening?

Tim Leary (Peter Pan) where hast thou flown?
And Eldridge Cleaver, with thy pants with cleavage,
dost thou hear God--and not thy people moan?
O Kesey, have thy Merry Pranksters nudged
the bucket once too often? Angela Davis,
now hast thou tenure, and so will not be budged?
Bob Dylan, art thou bloated now as Elvis?
Was it Reverend Jim thou once called Mr. Jones?
And Jud, sour Jonah who cried doom upon us,
hast thou left Nineveh to plow the stones?

Life will do anything that doesn't *not* work,
so beauty leaks like love, like water, through
the darkest soil or weighs the trees with ice.
We do what we must. We do a great deal more.
Excess of spirit, like our prodigal sperm,
sways in romance or madness, boils our dreams,
and swells the pupa till it bursts its seams
and wild imago crawling sticky out
stretches and airs its gaudy wanton wings
in the spring sun, so aimlessly to fly,
waver and breed in vanity, and die.
The throat that feeds is also the throat that sings.

This is the revolution, this slow turning,
this riding of the mountain round through winter,
these dormant seeds, this quiet compost burning,
this editing of copy for the printer,
this holding hands in silence round the table,
this tender loving that makes loving tough,
stretching our limits far as we are able,
knowing enough is enough--and never enough.

1969-1979

This section covers ten years instead of five because I wasn't writing much poetry between 1969 and 1973. In my new role as social activist I was running around gathering material for and spending my home hours writing *Culture Out of Anarchy: the Reconstruction of American Higher Learning* and *Families of Eden: Communes and t':e New Anarchism*. The poetry begins again with Jenny in 1970. After years of frustrating experiences in various day programs we decided that year to place her in a residential school--Camphill. "The Village" tells of this family experience and the decision which has affected our lives since. I took terminal leave from Antioch to study communes--knowing we wanted to join or start one. We bought this hundred acres we named Downhill Farm in November, 1971, and people started moving in. We joined them the next summer.

Part of my removal from the system was an increasing disregard for the whole world of publishing. "The Village" was rejected by all the trade and literary magazines and published by a little (short-lived) commune magazine. Okay, so I would write for commune magazines. For the most part I have not submitted work in the last ten years to other than the publications of the counterculture. "Homage to Shakespeare" is an indulgence of this retirement. Though I included three sonnets published in the early sixties (#42 and 43 in *The Nation*, #26 in *Harper's*), the rest have not yet been sent to magazines and they have had, in fact, few readers. I have come to think of my poetry as a kind of message in a bottle, which I hope someday drifts ashore.

As I mentioned in the last note, a number of the "Rumors" were written during this period. I have written family poems all my life, but rarely saved them--here I have a few. Sometimes I think Myrtle is a better poet than I am, so I included her works. This period takes you from the middle-class insouciance of "Easing In During the Late Show" to the communal terrors of "Perhaps an Owl" and expansion of "Triad." In my mind that is a kind of progress.

THE VILLAGE

i. Saturday

Tomorrow we take her to the village.
                          A sturdy seven,
Jenny is oval of face, her small eyes darting mischief.
She looks sideways, teasing, giggling,
                          her few words
arduous grunts and squeals. She runs tottery, trounces
her little brother.
              The moment swells, a translucent balloon
before her eyes, the past *gone gone,* the future like
Good Humor meltingly offered, just beyond grasp.
                                        About
tomorrow, she knows her clothes, toys, books, are packed in boxes.
I stand at my study door.
                    Outside she swings on a rope
from the oak, happiest by herself.
                          The neighbor children
cannot understand her. They are brain damaged.
We who lean on tomorrow do not understand.

ii. Sunday

All of us edgy to leave,
                    Jenny goes out to wait
in the car, flies back flatfooted running ponytail swinging
to fetch her yellow lunchbox. One doesn't go to school
without a peanut butter sandwich.
                          We laugh and load
for the family trip through rolling Pennsylvania,
three hours of autumn, Jenny hooting gladly, pointing
at passing trucks, ponds, cows.
                          She pulls her mother's chin
around to be sure she is getting through.
                                And when we find

the gravel road to the village,

the cottage assigned,

she knows.

Wing wing! she shouts, and scrambles out to try

the swing
by the door.

Adults fumble through introductions while
she darts into bedrooms, bathroom, locates piano and toys,
riding her moment like a surfer, carrying her
essential world in her head.

It is distressingly
simple. We invent anxieties about
her toilet, sleep, food, language.

It seems as though there ought
to be more papers to shuffle. Even death requires
more preparation.

We leave,

the car vacant and still.

iii. the village

Stupid means nothing in nature; you are what you are.

Jacques Cousteau

Driving away, my mind plays tricks:

Suppose there were
a village

just for people who lived in care

of one
another, where

differences were expected.

Judge
not.

With what one has, make do.

I see a village
spreading its cottages and economical gardens
on the verdant hills,

people sharing whatever,

coming

together to work, play, learn, worship, in joy.
                                        No last
names.
          Ages all relative.
                    The sexes mingling.
                                        The point
of life being
               nurture, fulfillment, happiness.
I try to imagine yearning for nothing, having enough
food, warmth, company,
                    reading no ads.
                                   Imagine making
our own music, bread, and love.
                         Have we brains enough among us?
Imagine congruence of need and delight.
                                        Imagine
sinking into the downy bed of the earth's abundance,
letting now be adequate.
                    There is nothing but now.
I dream a village
               rooted and spreading,
                                   ready
for seasons,
          riding the earth round steadily into
the dawn.
               *   *   *
          We are excluded.
                         On the freeway speeding,
cursed with the knowledge of our own mortality,
striving against that limit,
                    believing a living is
something to be earned,
                    memory clogged with guilt,
future a terror,
               present a point of balance we
have lost.
               *   *   *
          There they believe inside each one is one

dwelling in splendor,
                    beyond all damage,
                                        beyond all
distinctions,
                free of the yoke of time--
                                    a self, a presence.
(I speak with eyes to her in there: hello Jenny.)
There they believe the body with its senses,
                                            mind
with sense,
                are tricks of light on the face of the troubled pool.
I try to imagine believing: Flesh is not me. I am not
a sum of deeds.
                These very thoughts are a mere flux
of current.
                I cannot think my way to the still depths.
                    *   *   *
We are excluded.
                    We are normal.
                                    We would be bored
in that village.
                We would organize it for profit.

iv. Monday

We rearrange the house. It is strangely quiet without
her random energy careening through the day.
The night is undisturbed.
                        We are guiltily relieved
of soiled pants, clutter, spills, howls, fights, blaring TV.
Things put away stay put away.
                            Jenny is guiltless,
rolling her day before her like a ball.
                                    We call
to find she loved the school, slept well. They are overwhelmed
by her relentless curiosity.
                        I smile,

knowing they will be won, wryly knowing the bother,
exasperation, weariness, the worry.
                                    (When sick,
she lies so wordless in her body,
                                    rapidly breathing.)
Knowing the lesson she teaches in unconditional love.
At home we look at one another newly.
                                    There is
much we have neglected between us, much we have
poured in a bottomless receptacle, much
to be built.
            In us are planted Jenny's slanted humor,
trust, and desperate vitality.
                                We search
out innocent ground, the place, the friends, the strength
                                                to farm.

EASING IN DURING THE LATE SHOW

It's all right
          wanting it this way that way, even not
wanting it's all right (though I'd rather you not want me
not to want it).
          I've checked around, and it's all right
black white old young fat thin, even (as we are) being
thickly forty, muscles giving way
                    boing! twang! like
rotting straps. (I studied our bodies in the long mirror
in the bathroom. They're all right.)
                    Some get their kicks being
faithful unfaithful desired desiring undesired.
Some feel guilty all the time,
                    or inadequate,
which is a drag for them and others, but if that
is what they can't help feeling,
                    I guess it's all right.
Some object
          to being used as objects.
                    I kind
of like being used,
               but if they want to hang their egos
on it that's all right with me.
                    It's difficult
in the bathtub or generally under water.
                    On the grass in the rain
it's fine, but itchy after.
                    On the rug by the fire it's splendid
if the kids don't come downstairs.
                    (The woods are overrated.)
Surreptitious is fun (notes, winks, squeezes under

tables, afternoons, no squeaking--
                              sneaking home).
Flagrancy is also fun
                    (orgies, everybody flopping
around, switching, pot, AC-DC, the works--
                                        sounds
great, but I've not had the opportunity to).
Romantic is all right (dress, go out, theater,
maybe the Bahamas--
                  though I can't see it adds that much).
In fact, in spite of
                    revolution and the dis-
approval of the young and its being
middleclass unintellectual inartistic and socially unconscious
while the new world blooms around us like dogwood in the bracken,
it's all right, just us,
                      our bed in the suburbs,
                                            bourbon
and flicker of the set.
                      Hard to believe that home
is best,
        but I've found no improvement on your nudging
back in my lap, just lolling along
                                (even dozing, even
stopping to potty the boy,
                        no sweat,
                                there's always more
where that came from).
                      Come once twice don't come,
                                              it's all right,
drawing it out like taffy,
                        and if you fantacize
on Joseph Cotten's monotone,
                          that's you,
                                    and it's all right.

UNCLE MORTIMER'S THEORY

Uncle Mortimer had a theory there's nothing sacred
which he set out to prove.
                    Ate his way like a weevil
through family business law church the Masons and three
wives before I got to know him.
                    I don't trust you
Uncle Mortimer I said and he said I had good reason,
laughing and returning my pewter ashtray from
his pocket to the table. Don't turn your back he said
I like you.
                    Then get your hand out of my crotch I said.
Is nothing sacred?
                    I suppose that you're inviolate?
Very nearly, I said, at least selective.
                                        Values said
Uncle Mortimer philosophically are all
subjective. You show me any real reason to
refrain from anything or for that matter to
do anything, I'll show you a game, the rules
like fences in your head--Blake's mind-forged manacles--
he said, blowing his nose on a flag he carried for that
purpose.
                    I couldn't live without those fences I told him.
More likely you couldn't die. I have nothing to die for.
People are always making contracts, you poets for instance
twist everything you want to say to make it fit
some arbitrary form. People are always building
altars to sacrifice their Isaacs on. People
are always organizing clubs to keep other
people out of, always drawing boundaries
saying MINE. Well property is theft. If you
really want to end war crime racism injustice

just remember one man's sacred cow is another's
beefsteak.
                    It won't work I said.
                                        Well you just tell me
what does? You think if we just keep on pulling up
and putting fences in we'll finally get it right?
                                                        Well
what about your theory nothing's sacred? I
asked him.
                    What about it?
                                        I mean suppose it's wrong.
Suppose I went over to that bureau drawer and pulled
out something sacred and you saw it and knew right then
it really was?
                    He watched me warily.
                                        Don't worry
I said I wouldn't. I don't trust you and besides
the bureau drawer's not where I keep it, but suppose.

You're lying! he screamed
                            and clutched his sacred theory close.
I don't trust you! he screamed
                            and fled into the night.

BETH AT SEVENTEEN

You are a morning without alarm
   when sinking back into the undersea of dream
     and amniotic warm
is no more nor less entreating than
   the thrill of rising.

You are that brazen beam
   emerging through horizon clouds and spilling
     laughter from open arms,
surging as the world turns, even
   and effortless in your diurnal calm,
     moving
       the way the stars run.

You are dew-weighted May bending
   with beatific grace, yet standing,
     joy running in your stem.
Yours is the loving sadness of the dawn,
   and its silent song.

Day's turbulence you contain,
   and memory of midnight dungeon,
and yet you stun us with your rising, easy rising,
   glad as morning and forgiving
     as the spring.

WHY THE FACTORY STOPPED

Not the workers picketing, taking turns carrying signs
and playing pinochle. Who needs workers?
                                          Not the poor
rioting and looting outside the high barbed wire.
The college students did not stop the factory. They
sat non-negotiably for months in the dean's office. Who
needs deans?
           It was not the ecologist, turning up his nose
where the factory leaked in the river, spewed its flatulence
from tall chimneys, though the ecologist did pick up a plethora
of beercans and condoms from the beaches.
                                         Revolutionaries
blowing up scholars did not stop it, and the Third World
starved angrily in vain.
                        The greying liberals in
dashikis never stopped anything.
                                It was not the war nor
the cessation thereof. The stock market traded and traded,
nothing changed. The liberated women burned
bras right and left, the Panthers offed a pig, and Hell's
Angels gangbanged Shirley Temple Black to no avail.

It was the executives, believed their own advertising.
What you going to do, you come home every night
to sex in living color, everyone screaming at you
Consume Consume, who needs to go to work?
                                           It was
managers turned on to Wrigleys, extending coffee breaks
forever.
        It was the man with the keys, one morning took
a left off the freeway. He's now
                                 in Marlborough Country.

THE PERVERT

Before you love me, let me say . . .

Don't say it.
I love you for what you are. I don't need words.
But you should know that when consumed by passion
I sometimes have an uncontrollable urge . . . .

Don't say it. What seems right to you will surely
seem right to me--and, well, if not, I may
silently signal in the dark. Don't spoil it
by talk about it in the light of day.

But you were talking about it at the table
with friends who read about it in a book.
You mean . . . ?
                    Yes, that's exactly what I mean.
Why did you have to say it?
                         Darling, look . . . .
I will not look! That sort of thing is not
the sort of thing we can talk about alone.

But, when consumed by passion, we may do it?
I'll scream. Such things are simply never done.

MYRTLE WHIMPLE'S SAMPLER

(her best-loved poems)

True Love

You'll know just when it's happening:
  Your tummy starts to flutter,
And ever time you think of him
  Your kneejoints melt like butter,
And when he calls, why, Sakes alive!
  Your heart is in your mouth,
And all the blood has left your head
  And flowed down to the South,
And words won't come, your throat just gurgles
  Like an airlock in a sewer.
When that's the way your feelings feel,
  You know your love is pure.

Say you're standing washing dishes
  Up to elbows in the sink,
And you scrub off all the daisies,
  And the toaster starts to stink,
And the water's cold and greasy,
  Yet you stare into the alley
Just dreaming of a golden Prince
  Aboard a golden galley.
Your mom may think you're looney
  And your pa yells, "Land Above!"
But you can't tell them, can you,
  That your malady is love?

Well, your teacher knows geometry,
  But you know more than she.
And the cop don't like the way you parked,

But you just think, "La dee dee."
And Pa don't like your hose and bras
  Hanging dripping into the tub,
And Ma don't like the radio
  Making such a loud hubbub,
And no one understands you. No,
  They haven't got a clue,
For you know one thing they don't know:
  This time your love is true.

A Daddy's Love

How does a little girl learn of love?
  From her daddy, still and strong.
On Sundays he goes fishing,
  And he lets her tag along.

"Why are you digging, Daddy?"
  He never says a thing,
But scoops the worms into the can--
  His way of answering.

"Don't stay out late," calls Mommy.
  He lights up his cigar.
"Remember that child's bedtime!"
  He simply starts the car.

He lets her watch him thread the worm
  Wiggling on the hook
And cast the weighted, baited line
  Into the dark brown brook,

And when the cork is floating free,
  And all is under control,
He takes his bottle from his pocket
  And lets her hold the pole.

But when the cork goes under hard,
  He grabs the pole again,
Jerks, cusses at the naked hook--
  For that is work for men.

Then when she has to wee wee he
  Directs her to the bushes,
And when she tries to talk to him,
  Finger to lip, he shushes.

All afternoon in silence they
  Sit and don't scare the fish,
And though they don't catch any, it's
  All that a girl could wish

To sit beside her daddy and
  To help him home at night
And drift away to dreamland
  Hearing her parents fight,

Learning that hugs and kisses are
  Just not her daddy's way,
And you can be sure he loves you most
  When he has least to say.

Mother's Love

Now I have watched my children grow up and turn away
And oftentimes neglect me and hear not what I say,
But pout and sass and roll their eyes to God above,
And know it may take years before they value Mother's love.
But inwardly I smile and wait. In time they'll see
How right I was, how much they learned, at Mother's knee.

First word I learned was *Nasty,* for my Mother taught
Us kids what not to put our fingers in. We fought
and disobeyed and thought our Mother was just mean,
but when we go to Heaven, God knows that we'll be clean.
We learned our manners, kept our bodies out of sight,
For folks forgive most anything when people are polite.

But most of all a growing girl goes through a change
When womanhood descends, and her body gets all strange,
She needs her Mother--though advice is hard to take,
For then she's thinking time has come to make a break.
You bet I learned, although I chafed against the halter.
By sixteen I knew how to get Bert to the altar.

Oh Mother, I remember you caught me squeezing pimples
And slapped my fanny, smiled, winked, and pinched my dimples.
I know you read my diary and found Sen-Sen in my purse,
And whatever I might tell, you thought the truth was worse;
But though you always seemed to me so harsh and cold,
I know you loved me, Mother, now that I am old.

The Little Boy You Are To Me

With thinning hair and talk of stocks and bonds
And griping about the cost of your children's braces,
You kiss me with whiskey breath, and soon are gone,
A stranger in your home, yet there are traces
Around your eyes of a younger face I see:
    Georgie, you're still a little boy to me.

The bannister still wobbles from your sliding;
Your swastika scratched in cement is on the porch.
Your basketball hoop rusts on the garage.
The dining table bears a soldering scorch.

From memories you are a refugee,
  But George, you're still a little boy to me.

You now use words for which I washed your mouth
and pop your knuckles, looking the other way,
And bite your nails, and yet I hold my tongue.
I hope you change your underwear every day
And your wife cares enough to check and see--
  Though for her you're not the boy you are for me.

Oh, with what freckly cheeks and mischievous eyes
You looked up when I caught you with the milk money!
How you played sick to keep from going to school,
Coating each little lie with words of honey!
You think you fool me now, son? Fiddle-dee-dee!
  Remember, you're just a little boy to me.

Yes, I know you tried to call me on my birthday.
My phone was out-of-order? Yes, I'm sure.
The florist gypped you, failing to deliver?
Your wife's illness only you can cure?
George, don't forget what a Mother's love can see:
  The naked little boy you are to me.

Ballad of the Check-Out Girl

That store was like an oven
  In August of forty-two,
But Bert had gone to be a soldier,
  So I did my duty, too.

The manager of A.& P.
  Had put in new machines
And needed high-school graduates
  To learn the new routines.

Well, I never finished high school
    But married Bert instead.
"Two children are the equivalent,"
    The A.& P. manager said.

He taught us how to pull the tray
    And read the numbers right
But add a penny here and there
    If we were quick and bright.

And how to pack the paper bags
    With canned goods on the bottom.
He fired three girls the first week
    Who couldn't learn what he taught 'em.

I didn't flirt with 4-F's
    Or gossip with the girls
Buying their movie magazines
    With rollers in their curls.

We weighed and sacked the vegetables:
    There was no such thing as plastic.
For meat we counted ration stamps.
    I tell you, things were drastic!

So while our boys protected us
    By fighting overseas,
Some of us were behind the line
    Busily punching keys,

Snapping gum and counting cartons,
    Three for thirty-nine,
Dreaming that when our men came home
    Then we could wine and dine.

I sneered at Sue at the next counter
  (Her voice could surely rankle)
Feeling my veins grow varicose
  Around each ankle.

Now when I see the blank-faced young
  In our air-conditioned store,
I'd like to shake them up and tell
  How we girls won the war.

Guardian of the Highway

Cousins and kids, all gather round
For Uncle Erasmus has come to town,
The mystery man, Aunt Tilly's pride
She talks about, but seems to hide,
Now out of the darkness, out of the cold,
With tales to tell of the open road.
So turn off the TV, put out the dog,
Turn on the gas for the Permalog,
And gather round your Uncle's knees,
And he will tell, if you say please,
Adventures bold in No-Man's Land:
  For Uncle Ras is a Toll-Booth man.

How does he get there? How does he leave?
What are his joys? What's his pet peeve?
Who does he talk to? What does he say?
Does he prefer working night or day?
Do drivers ever do things strange?
How big a bill has he had to change?
Does he ever sit? Does he ever smile?
Does he go to the bathroom once in a while?
Does he close up his window in a storm?
Has he ever worn out a uniform?
Just try to imagine, if you can
  Tales to be told by a Toll-Booth man!

Once Uncle Ras was a boy like you
And dreamed of doing things men do:
Fly a plane or put out fires,
Capture crooks, put on snow tires,
Stick needles into people's arms,
Buy mineral rights from failing farms,
Climb poles to plug in telephones,
Make dinosaurs out of old bones--
Such occupations are not rare,
But one in a million has a flair.
What made Ras change his whole life plan
    And choose to become a Toll-Booth man?

So gather round and you shall learn
The secret urge that deep did burn
And made Ras stand out from the herd,
Hearing a call few ever heard
To learn the craft and Stoic art
To take his post and stand apart
Through rain and sleet and snow and hail
To gather coins and lift the rail
For car or camper, truck or bus,
Opening the road--and all for us!
Ras never joins the caravan,
    But stays behind: the Toll-Booth man!

The Funeral in the Rain

All is forgiven, Hilda Jean,
    As we lower you into sod--
The preacher and I in falling rain,
    Sending you to God.

But I can see your spirit rise
    Above to greener pastures
And smile as I remember your
    Puppyhood disasters.

Born anew, will you again
   Chew on heavenly shoes?
And on those sainted carpets leave
   Your inimitable pooh-poohs?

Methinks I see the blazing light
   Around the golden throne
And hear from under it the crunch
   As you gnaw on a bone.

Perhaps Our Father takes you up
   To give you a manna-scrap.
Oh, Hilda Jean, I hope you won't
   Piddle in His lap!

I know the Lord has sympathy,
   Gives no unkind rebuke,
But even I sometimes got cross
   To find another puke.

But what a watchdog you will make,
   Relentless in your labors,
Wearing a path along the fence
   Yapping at Hellish neighbors!

The angels will watch over you
   When love begins to bloom
And, as your careful Mumsy did,
   Drive males off with a broom.

When you grew old and sick and whined
   And seemed to get no better
I put castor oil in your Friskies and
   Knitted you a sweater

288

To no avail: the hand of Time
    Throttled you in your sleep.
The silence now when friends arrive
    Almost makes me weep.

But in those blessed realms above
    You'll join the angels' choir
And howl throughout eternity
    Where terriers never tire!

A Rhyme in Time
(for my grandaughter, Patti Lorelei, who, assigned
to write a poem for her fifth-grade composition class,
said she couldn't think of one.)

If you've got to write a poem,
    And you haven't got a thought,
And your tummy's got the jitters,
    And your tongue in throat is caught,
And your brow is sort of sweaty,
    And your hand can't make a start,
There is just one place to find a poem:
    Child, look into your heart.

Sometimes a piece of paper can
    Seem blank and.hard as stone,
And the pencil you pick up to use
    Seems blunt as any bone,
And the words that came so easy when
    You were talkin' on the phone
All scattered like the blackbirds that
    Left the king alone,
And you're sittin' there all bound and gagged,
    Your senses blown apart.

There's only one thing left to do:
Child, look into your heart.

I know you are too big to cry
And much too nice to curse:
Just listen to your quiet heart
A-pumpin' out a verse.
No need to bite your pencil or
To pout and make a frown.
Inside you is a ticker that
Will never let you down,
That will straighten out your tangles,
Put your horse before its cart,
And flood your emptiness with song:
Child, look into your heart.

Christmas Letter

Hi folks! The price of cards this year
Sent me to the mimeograph
At the church to bring you up to date
And give you all a laugh.

Since Bert went on to his reward
The house has been unpainted.
I priced aluminum siding, but,
I tell you, nearly fainted.

Otherwise just fine, the mortgage paid
(No big bad bank to bite us).
Just living till eligible for Medicare
To tend to this arthritis.

My mailbox stands with hungry mouth.
Phone stares with a gloomy squint.
Thank God for my independence,
But not too much (hint, hint).

Jill wrote that Clyde had broke his leg
When his bike took a nasty spill.
But that was last summer. I haven't heard,
But by now he's surely well.

Andy, I hear, has a new job--
taking the family to Kuwait.
That's in Africa or somewhere hot.
Maybe Martha will lose weight.

Jock's still in college--for his sixth year!
Don't know when he will return.
Either they've got a godawful lot to teach
Or he's mighty slow to learn.

I don't think any of you know
Uncle Seth on my father's side
Who was a railroad clerk in Orlando?
Well, anyway, he died.

That avocado seed I started
Labor Day before last
Fills up the dining alcove window
and picks up my breakfast.

Lots of goings-on at the church these days--
Things I best not mention here--
But you-know-who's on the Building Committee
And on the dirt has kept an ear.

Remember Mr. Weiner down the block?
Well, widowers reach a certain silly stage.
Imagine--hosiery out on his line!
Can't he pick on someone his own age?

Stockings remind me of Christmas and
The cheer I wish you all.
If Santa don't visit I hope he has
The decency to call.

                    Love,
                    Myrtle

There's Always God

In the depths of my depression,
  Which my pills won't touch,
    Feeling lonely and rejected and abused--
For instance, by the plumber,
  Who charges far too much,
    And I'll never buy another car used--
When my hair is grey and thinning,
  And it won't hold a wave,
    And my children haven't written since November,
Then I think about the government
  And nearly want to rave,
    But just in time I remember
That when everything is hopeless,
  Or at least extremely odd,
    There's always God:

Someone to comfort me and listen,
  And not tell me His troubles,
    Who feels about taxes as I do,
Who tells me not to worry,

That a watched pot never bubbles,
  So I shouldn't work myself into a stew.
We dawdle over coffee,
  And watch *The Eternal Light*.
    Down supermarket aisles I have a guide.
And when the drapes are drawn,
  And we settle for the night,
    I know that He will stay on His own side.
For when I need a Shepherd
  Who knows where to keep His rod,
    There's always God.

So if life's to you a mystery,
  An endless masquerade,
    And you have to play a part in this Who-done-it,
If church is just a Bingo game
  Eternally played,
    And you always bought a card and never won it,
If mankind just distresses you
  With wars and treachery
    And yet it seems to you you have no choice,
If you have put your two bits in
  On pollution and lechery
    Until it seems that you have lost your voice,
If yet you yearn to tread new waters,
  Waters never trod--
    There's always God.

Ode to Henry Kissinger

What a blessed gift to this strife-torn world
You gave us when around it you whirled
Following the commands of our President Nixon
As though you were Prancer, Dancer and Vixen,
Making friends of all our old enemies,
For all our problems finding new remedies,

Here and there like a half-dozen Hanks,
For which we now give you our heartfelt thanks.

But why when they gave you the Nobel Prize
Did you share it with a Communist we all despise?
You must have choked back a bitter tear
To see half the limelight go to that queer!
But you bore the insult in silence like a man,
Knowing your friends back home would understand.
Besides, you already had your mind on the Arabs and oil
And were figuring out ways the Jews you might foil.

God Bless you Henry Kissinger, where're you may roam,
And this message of love from each red, white and blue home
Is a greater reward than that prize in Stockholm,
Because you know we mean it and are ever true
To the might and the power of the red, white and blue,
And this night of peace when our Savior was born
We'll remember how H.K. weathered their scorn.
It is not Santa Claus we see fly through the air,
But Henry Kissinger, through the rockets' red glare,
Bringing PEACE to the WORLD, though the Communists stare!

BIRDS AND BEES

You know how, mornings, you jiggle the bed till the nails squeak,
and your penis stands up, and you just can't make it go down,
and it feels so good you can't stop even though it hurts,
and finally you come to our room and ask with a frown,

"What makes it do that?" and I get out of bed, and mine too
is waving and nodding and throbbing in stately style
(because before you came in your mama and I
had been hunching under the covers for some little while),

and I say it's nothing to worry about, but you worry,
and can tell by the way that I say it that I worry, too,
can tell that I know a lot more about this whole problem
than anyone ever seems willing to speak of with you?

And you know what Josh and Rachel asked you this morning
(since they are just five and three, and you're all of nine,
and they look up to you to tell them what grownups will never
explain, though they beg them, and stomp their feet, and whine)?

What they wanted to know was exactly how girls make babies,
and you said boys did it to them, but you didn't know how.
I could tell by the way that you glanced up at me that really
what you didn't know was how much adults would allow

children to say about questions that come to their minds.
Well, you know how in otherwise interesting TV shows
a woman and man sometimes kiss--and you turn away?
Why *is* it we hide from and whisper what everyone knows?

You know how our roosters ride piggy-back on the hens,
and the dogs sniff and mount any lady dog who arrives,
and how dragonflies mate in midair, and our buck goat snickers
and pees in his beard to please his adoring wives?

Well, yes, that's how boys help girls have their babies.
They put in their thing and jiggle around till it spurts,
and it feels good even if they don't want any babies.
But we don't talk about it--and that is mostly what hurts.

KING OF THE MOUNTAIN

At last to stand on the grassy knoll above
the sprawling mass, the shouts and sweat, the crush,
to have bubbled to the top of the sticky broth,

to endure that midst of elbows, scrambling drove,
to tug at garments, fling anonymous flesh,
then momentarily float there, free as froth--

unnecessary, light, luxurious,
salty and cool in the tongues of evening air,
while parents in their dim surrounding houses
digest their dinners, placid, unaware

that a featherweight, by accident or stealth,
defying muscle and justice, now from limbo,
is silhouetted, catching a casual breath,
surveying his dominion, arms akimbo.

OUR FORTY-SIXTH MOTHER'S DAY

You are about me like May morning air,
your softly knobby fingers poking these keys,
your tongue enjoying one last cup before
the house arises to the day's confusion.

At our age we are ageless, genderless,
trading dependencies and strengths like clothes.
Those twenty years must once have seemed a veil
through which you could not see yourself in me,
close in your girl's arms, but in a dimple,
and all I saw of you was giant nipple.
But now our lines converge; the end is common.
One and another mothers the other's manhood
in silence over all the years and miles.

You ride the forest trails with me on horseback,
and stake tomatoes, weed the onions, watch
a pair of cardinals at the feeder taking
their timid turns. Last night at sunset while
the hard hills softened into mist we heard
wild turkeys gobble in the valley, and
the seasoning seeped in our veins of old
thanksgivings, times outside of time, evenings
that ever gently die and then recur.

Five lines have sprung from mine, from ours, and each
like a stubborn weed of some Southwestern strain
asserts its independence of all nurture,
stretching its own green vine, replete with thorns.
I try to remember how you allowed that growth
and how it cut you, remember that your pride

could never be in worshipping resemblance
but in the sinew that sustained all difference,
glad as it twisted, rambled: "Just don't whine."

Each time I wince and sigh and try to keep
from interfering, I think of how you must have
ached and yet refrained. I thank you for
the things you did not save me from: They saved me.
That is the heritage I can pass on
and watch ironically how after all
the breed affirms its strength in spite of wild
diversion: Our pictures show us all alike.

AFTER HARD RIDING

It's hard to love a horse. There is no way
to hug him and express your tenderness.
Kissing is out of the question. You cannot say
a thing he will believe--in speech, much less
in poetry. When choked with vision, humor,
dreams, yearning in twilight to share a misty mood,
one's touch will be flicked off like a fly or rumor--
unless the hand that reaches holds some food.
No access to the heart beneath that brawn
nor to the fancies that bone brow encloses.
You drop the reins. He munches on the lawn.
Unsaddle. Vainly stand there, rubbing noses.
   When I am horse to you, or you to me,
   we ride together hard--and lovingly.

PERHAPS AN OWL

"Did you hear that screaming in the night?" you ask
me at breakfast. "It was probably an owl--
once, then again, again, not regular
as an animal, not shrill, not quite a howl.
We were holding hands. I waited waited, thinking
you were hushed (it was so distant) waiting, too.
The dogs were still. Perhaps some cry of mating
or terror, pain, some hunting screech--not human,
unless, of course, I thought, it was he alone.
(I remembered at dinner his eyes like dusty gems,
the scrape in his laugh. I thought I heard him moan.)
These warm March nights anything might be stirring
in the full moon, something on the prowl.
I should have turned on the light and read a book.
I'm sure it was nothing. Maybe it was an owl."

That time I slept, but I, too, have stared at the ceiling
or closed my eyes to witness bloody tableaus--
him stretched by his tipi fire, at last his knife
having found its way past ribs to sprout a rose.
Noises of birds and beasts still let one sleep.
On this dark and brambled mountain people are
what torment people--neighborly smiles by day;
by night mouse thoughts find bedded minds ajar.
People or fires--the fires that people cause--
these are the tongues that lick me to unrest.
Yes, better to read, to smoke, to have lights on:
If need be, meet the unknown fully dressed.
We lie so soft and naked in our darkness
while madness stalks and in the doorway stands.
Better to sleep, but if you must lie waking,
I'm glad I was there, that we were holding hands.

TRIAD

(a sonnet for Sandy and Marty)

I

Were yin yangless and yang yinless, two
(complementary as shoe to shoe)

would mirror in their teeter-totter love
the handy he inside the she, or glove.

II

But three, androgynous in limber strength,
endlessly braiding leather, cord and wire,
fulfill their space with depth and height and length,

each helping two, as three logs make a fire.
   Stable on rugged ground, our tripod stool
revolves without repeating, like a gyre,

tempering hot and cold to warm and cool,
yet catalyzing with a central rhyme
that stretches the measure and renews the rule

III

so skeletal space throbs with the blood of time.

A ROUGH AVERAGE

The normal person has a thought with some
sexual content every twenty-five
seconds on the average.

                              I drop the book
in my lap--which stirs awakened like a spring pond.
Research psychologists people my dream
as moles crisscross and hump the even lawn.

In unisex white coats they are strapping wires
to downy arms or watching telltale needles
twitch on the rolling sheet.

                         Tell us your thoughts.
That spasm of ink reads nine on the Richter scale.
What fault is slipping in your depths? What buckling
of which impinging continental plates?
Your resistant skin is damp with dewy beads.
Tell us,
              they whisper, probing like jealous mates.

I check the second hand and welling up
comes Beverly in a bikini, miles
from shore, leaning to leeward, snatching a patch
of seaweed with a boathook.

                         Look at the life!
She points to seething creatures dwelling among
the pale, air-pocketed tangle of stems and leaves:
shrimp, crabs, bugs--God knows what--a populous island.
But my eyes have sunk in tanned cleavage to
the secret edge of white. She and her husband
will never know my thoughts, which will not focus
on marine biology. I hear her words.
I will never know her thoughts.

                              Now the shovel

slices the tunnel of the city of worms.
Eyes glued to lens we witness venery.
The laboratory is all black and white,
but color squirms on the slide, squirms in our minds.
I am normal, I desperately say, but do not say
what the silent second hand seeks out and finds.

PSYCHOLOGY TODAY

My belly joined the Belly Potential Movement.
My brain took EST. My left eye last was seen
swimming with Swami Riva. My right was rolfed.

I'm actualized, if you know what I mean,
transcending, getting ready for the future,
fulfilled with helium, unstressed, piecemeal.

My organs drift asunder above the circus,
each bulbous with capacity to feel--
eastward the nose and south the probing tongue,

each toe afloat and powdered like a clown,
aurora borealis genitalia
higher than acupuncture can bring down.

Why then this aching? Surely not my soul--
for none was found when all was picked apart.
And, strings all cut, who would expect such throbbing

from one gland left on earth--my leaden heart?

AN APOSTATE YOGI

This yogi in his dhoti in Benares
stood on one leg.
One outstretched palm kept ice from melting
while the other fried an egg.
Wearing nothing but a turban and a mandala
he dwelt in a Frigidaire
eight months chewing a ginseng root.
They don't need air.
They are not dependent on the variables
that generally maintain us.
They show the autonomic nervous system who is boss.
A yogi can suck water up his anus,
swallow Kleenex and pull it out his nos.

A woman with a yogi for a lover
said he never came too soon,
yet sitting in his lotus with his thoughts on God
could spurt all afternoon.
I never met a lady yogi, but I hear they menstruate
when they please.
A yogi never laughs without deciding,
nor does he sneeze.
He makes his heart beat fast or slow, depending
on mind, not glands.
His hiccups, sweat and pupil sizes
obey commands.
He farts at will and never apologizes.

As a boy I tried to suck my belly under
ribs till I saw my spine.
Though I never tried a rope or cobra, I played
my ocarina for some twine.
I pounded blunt ten penny nails through plywood
and would have lain on it, no doubt,
if I could have got my weight all in one motion
evenly stretched out.
I wiggled my ears and pursed my sphincters,
crossing my eyes.
In school I sat with a stony gaze, engaged
in internal exercise.
But I surrendered as I aged

to the voluntary and involuntary
as discrete domains,
with uncontrollable regret.enduring
riot in my veins,
incontinently wishing I could master
that skill or art
that could predict, if not manipulate,
the weather of my heart.
And yet my effort is no more to strengthen,
but to subdue my will,
to go through ego's mirror and be whole.
Still you may see sitting very still,
straining to throw off the mind's control.

THE PEDDLER

I opened a stall in the market with many placards.
WISDOM I offered. Surely they need that.
WIT NEW AND SECONDHAND for lighter moments.
FLATTERY should sell out in nothing flat.

HARD WORK I thought was something the world wanted.
HONESTY--spice for the discerning few.
DIPLOMACY for those with much to lose.
For those with nothing I promised to be *TRUE*.

FACTS for skeptics, *FAITH* for mystics. *VISION*
for the undecided, also for the blind.
COMMITMENT for the serious, and for
the frivolous I had an *OPEN MIND*.

I had some *SKILL* and lots of *GOOD INTENTIONS*.
I knew *THE WAY*, but was *WILLING TO BE LED*.
I CAN BE HAD--a general sort of come-on.
Specifically, I added, *GOOD IN BED*.

IF YOU DON'T SEE WHAT YOU WANT JUST ASK,
EVERYTHING MUST GO INCLUDING ME.
JUST MAKE AN OFFER. I scratched that out: *DON'T BOTHER*.
STOCK, SHOP AND ONE SHOPKEEPER ALL FOR FREE.

But all the traffic passed me by, attracted
to a scrawny fellow with a screechy yelp
and scrawly note pinned to his scrap of jacket
pitifully announcing *I NEED HELP*.

And then one day a gorgeous buxom maiden
pulled up in a Rolls. She'd found just what she sought.
She wheedled me with molten eyes of love.
"All I want," she said, "is everything you've got."

I hastily packed my cases, closed my shutters,
crouched by the counter, waited for darkness, to flee.
People aren't to be trusted--especially people
who show any interest in the likes of me.

SATURDAY NIGHT, SUNDAY MORNING
(after reading Carl Sagan's Dragons of Eden*)*

In swamps of sleep my lizard brain arises,
coldbloodedly pursuing meal or mate,
spreads blooming throat or flicks tongue for a fly.
I am tense on the cliff. My scaly skin disguises
flitting of light nerve whips, my heart all bait.
I sleep erect with rapid rolling eye.

And then some trick of endrocrine imbalance
sends scarlet screams through limbic zones of panic
echoing down the stairwells of my head.
I love you--but my love is choked in silence.
My blistering tears are infantile and manic.
My dream rots soft--and poisonous with dread,

till neocortex army bugles bray
rescue around the rimrock of my skull
and savages fly naked to their caves.
I tie my tasteful tie the proper way
and in the mirror watch wild eyes grow dull,
blessing the God that slays me as He saves.

ALL THE SORE LOSERS

"You win," he said, and shrugged. She nodded,
in dark recesses chalking one more score.
   (A stave gave way in her corset, but
she thought she would not need it any more.)

   That night she took a torch, descending
by dripping stairs her endless, echoing halls.
   The flame was smoky, oily, but
gleamed on the trophies ranked along the walls.

Eight shapes of sweating brass were lovers
frozen in postures of athletic play,
   graceful, with swollen muscles, but
corroding here beyond the reach of day.

   Here were the scalps of ladies who
befriended her, and then revealed their faults.
   She bore their smiling manners, but
their stinking pelts now hung here in these vaults.

   A golden likeness of her daughter
evoked the time she found that trollop wrong.
   She had her son in silver, but
did he give up--or merely go along?

   With her husband she had taken pains
to get him, not at once, but piece by piece.
   Thus no one saw him suffer, but
grow daily leaner as she grew obese.

Now picking over his bone structure
she knew where he was fallible, joint by joint,
  so durable and pearly, but
he steadily surrendered, point by point,

  and now, she reckoned, had lost track
of all his losses and the total due.
  She cackled, counting. Time would prove
that she and she alone was right. She knew.

BELLS FOR JOHN CROWE RANSOM

  So gently he courted the world's body
  and wittily her flesh fused,
  she took him in before we were ready,
  leaving us bemused.

  From the tower where we went to ponder
  his ontological poses
  and listen for God's redeeming thunder,
  we saw him sprinkling roses

  and puttering round a tidy garden,
  picking beetles from potatoes,
  harvesting a bushel burden
  nothing like Plato's,

  a wiry gentleman in shirtsleeves
  so distant he seemed abstract,
  mulching young plants with dry old leaves
  on a quarter-acre tract.

  Hear then the bells at Gambier tolling,
  see family by the cold hearth,
  and us, descending slow and mulling
  how poetry finds earth.

LOVING MY ENEMIES

I must love my enemies: I have made
so many of them. Whether I, drowning, flailed
rescuers, or, terrier-nervous, yapped,
defending God knows what from God knows whom,
or thought I was the jester, licensed to wound,
I drove you all away. I wanted room

to grow my crooked stem, so sprouted thorns,
or, as self-consuming candle, blindly burned
in guttering isolation, or vacuum-drained--
as a black hole does the sky--all warmth and light.
Emperor of sunny nursery play,
I took all as due, nor wondered how or why.

Pursuit of justice was a good excuse
to wear the jackboots of some public cause
and stab a friend for a stranger's brief applause.
It simplified affection's murky snarl
to make such clean incisions. I have hurled
babies and bathwater out for a better world.

But mostly I won your enmity with love
too fast too soon, my overwhelming wave
of self too bountiful, too gladly given.
To save yourselves from my self you were driven
if not to anger to politic escape.
I said I love you: You foresaw a rape.

You must have loved me, enemies, to have left,
dreading the waste and smother of my gift,
sensing my naked need to be received.
Hard love withholds indulgence: You withheld.
Such closeness both of us would soon have scalded.
You could avoid what could not be repelled.

Safer, of course, to love thus at a distance--
a dream of faces gone, but nearly kissed--
blending across the years without resistance,
yin lost in yang, and none knows when or how.
But there is safety even in my bower,
for I love you still--but do not need you now.

FOR TOPHER AT ELEVEN

Like winter rye, you're pushing high,
   cleanly, in tender rush,
and I look on in cautious joy
   with love that makes you blush.

Your spears of innocence stand keen,
   gleaming in autumn dew,
as though the frost and hardening soil
   were meaningless to you.

Sap pulses through your limber stem
   as, pumping, unaware,
you suck from matted, reaching roots
   as delicate as hair

and drink the lean abundance of
   antique October's sun
and soak in earthy chemicals
   that make your juices run.

While morning moisture blows away
   you point into your noon
and stand all night responsive to
   the bulging harvest moon,

flashing your feather blades that cut
   their way into the air.
The edge of Now is all you know--
   inexhaustibly rare.

As one behind a window watching
　　foliage flame and fall,
warming his backside at the fire,
　　his spirit growing small

in readiness for ice to come,
　　I govern flesh with reason
while you spurt forth in naked green
　　defiance of the season.

Your lips now turn from my dry kiss
　　and your mind from what I know.
Hardest in autumn love is this:
　　the gift of letting go.

FOR KIRSTIN AT FIFTEEN

My not-quite-daughter, not-quite-woman, clearly not-quite-child, my not-quite-student, not-
quite-teacher, not-quite-partner, while this mere
moment of emanation trembles hot
as a bud that feels the friction of the flower
emerging from the stem, all gorged with June,
now let us celebrate your issuing hour--
when bloom that seems so tardy comes too soon.
I not-quite-want this moment to persist
and not-quite-wish it were already past.
I'm sure you don't quite know what might be missed
if either as child or woman you were classed.
　　Oh, rich ambivalence of maidenhood--
　　when every prospect seems an equal good!

312

FOR POLLY AT TWENTY

Look, Polly, in the mirror: see your father.
Even your good left hand is on the right.
That stub of nose and freckles once were his.
I hope his eyes still dance with that glad light.

When I was twenty I moved to Chicago
and faced a northern February blast.
I found the warmth I needed there in Marty--
one of the few things from those years to last.

Like you I left the nest as soon as able,
hitchhiked into the mountains at sixteen,
little and cute and scared and yet determined
to find out what my life and world might mean.

I, too, found safety on the fringe of risk,
using the little I had to the last ounce,
learning that, since I sometimes had to fall,
I should (1) not get too high; (2) learn to bounce.

You moved to Downhill Farm and took possession,
thriving in this life sooner than Marty and I,
sensing in bones still limber, heart still tender,
that a farm was incomplete without a Sky.

So if our conversations sometimes seem
the wordless clasp of complementing hands,
that is because so little needs explaining.
I grin. You grin. The mirror understands.

WHEN YOU SAID "ENOUGH"

Though all my life
should go to tatters as
the knees of jeans
grow grey,
then let through light,
then fray
beyond all patching,
still would I
remember how
blue as steel
and strong you made
me feel
last night.

BROOKLYN, 1979

Whitman, thou shouldst be living at this hour,
riding the Brooklyn subway or its cabs,
not tending wounds, but picking at the scabs
that crust our lives and turn our lifeblood sour.
The lusty laborers you knew now cower
in factories, kitchens, offices, or labs.
Their furtive hearts behind the concrete slabs
might yet find courage in your loving power.
O Walt, who reached into all secret places
unjudgingly and celebrated all,
now in this air-conditioned shopping mall
where buyers mingle masked, their features glossed,
discern our tender flesh and frightened faces
and whisper where our dignity was lost!

HOMAGE TO SHAKESPEARE
(work in progress)

1

True, I was tonguetied, as a peasant brought
into the Presence, that levee in your room,
my years of yearning fuming into thought
words would not fumble forth, nor dared presume.
Perfection in repose, an idle flower,
complete in self, you knew no want nor need,
sumptuously wasting morning's golden hour,
containing like a secret evening's seed.
And I, so much the elder, felt the younger,
sweatlocked and swelling, unable yet to crest,
starving for some still moment when no hunger
would lure me on in vain and anguished quest.
    But had I words, they would have named this grief:
    Age knows the blossom's endless hour is brief.

2

I dreamed an edifice of marble stood
at issue of an ancient avenue--
moonlit and silent, beyond all likelihood
the tomb or temple of some old Hindoo.
Long had I thrashed through woods so dark and thick
this vision struck me with the loving fear
that overwhelms a stumbling heretic
who finds the Way, and knows the Way is clear.
Now have I entered all those vacant rooms,
pattered impatient down those polished halls,
caressed the sculpture's alabaster blooms
and heard the music of my echoed calls.
    The Idol in the depths has had my kiss.
    Was this the Way? And has it come to this?

3

Enjoined from joining or from giving name
to love you drink so freely from my eyes,
I send you thoughts unseen, unheard, the same
as ghosts whose sight you dread, words you despise.
Beauty defined will disappear in blush,
and brilliance noted quickly pales and hides.
I learn the poetry of clarion hush
to fill the air where mystery abides.
But how can you know silence from neglect,
or from my absence know my presence waits?
Denied my tongue, and by injunction checked,
I fear that love unrealized abates.
      If the invisible Word a Son may seal,
      perhaps these Sonnets can make my love real.

4

What if old Time our hairy fathers made
capriciously, with no clear end in view,
then cackled as they toiled in long charade,
making up meanings she would straight undo?
What if she,like a cranky child, knocks all
stacked blocks into a random distribution,
allows empires to rise so they may fall,
and cancels with an R our evolution?
Might she not happen, in her savage play,
upon Perfection she did not intend,
and, recognizing that, in triumph say,
"This was the purpose, and this is the end"?
      What if she brought the old game to a halt,
      finding she had made *you* without a fault?

5

Finding she had made you without a fault,
Old Time, descending from her high divan
and ceasing to defile, maim and assault,
would play with and adore her perfect man.
This world would slumber in the hushed respite
from thunderous ticking of relentless clocks
while Time sat stunned in paralyzed delight
and dallied with her timeless paradox:
For you, the product of her labors, are
her confutation and her sole defeat,
her incarnation and her avatar,
quelling her appetite with cloying sweet.
   She dreams benignly only in my dream;
   I wake a native in Time's dread regime.

6

I wake a native in Time's dread regime
where the gavel cracks, and there is no appeal,
no damming nor diverting of the stream
nor any turning backward of the wheel.
I've seen a dancer make an arcing leap
and seem to rest a moment in the air.
Just such a moment may you beauty keep
and stay one floating instant unaware.
Waking, I would alert you, but I pause,
for fear of spoiling that *jeté* sublime,
and stand enraptured, knowing what grave laws
resist your flight. There is no pause in Time.
   Perfection is evasion of the clock
   that flourishes between a tick and tock.

7

As winter's placid snow in spring gives way
to squirming tentacles of surging life,
and spring surrenders to rank summer's sway,
which falls in turn to autumn's reaping knife,
so households heave with birth that rends their peace,
and toddlers topple tables, breaking glass,
then youths ferment in schoolrooms for release
till age ensues--wealth, waists and words amass.
Now weightless as a man in space, you seem
to drift in freedom where there is no ground.
Caught in such vacant sleep, you hardly dream
how swift you, willy-nilly, orbit round,
   but you are bound upon the wheel of seasons
   that neither spares your grace nor heeds your reasons.

8

Deeper than words comes music like a fin,
slicing the darkest waters of our souls.
Higher than words flies that wild violin
beyond this dreary world the mind controls.
Such fevered lonely hours have I lain,
nursing my sorrow like a chill bare sword,
tuning my nerves to some symphonic pain
that put my own to naught with strange discord.
You will not venture with me to that space
where jarring spheres coherent concord sing,
resolving treble dissonance with bass,
all harshness into sweetness gathering.
   You turn my music off because you fear
   you might not hear such tones--or, worse, might hear.

9

You primp before your mirror with such care
as a roustabout takes to become a Fool,
rendering your face a reverent stare
as though you had found godhead in a pool.
Nor paint nor comb nor tweezers can improve
what Nature gave her most artistic touch.
Unless you from the altar choose to move,
the congregation cannot worship much.
But if you look behind you in the glass
you see me waiting, looking at your rear.
Oh, turn, and you will seem much less an ass,
and find a mirror in which you appear
   more truly than in silver's cheap reflection:
   My eyes alone can show your full perfection.

10

That mirror's face, left-handed complement,
sight's echo from the void, appears to flatter,
but mocks the man it seems to represent,
love's parity, fleshed out in antimatter.
The universe is filled, or so they say,
with everything reversed in symmetry
except the processes of slow decay--
through which Time leaches all in entropy.
Turn to the window, glass that best reveals
the transient beauty of true flesh and blood.
This glass gives vent to what the other seals:
our floating moment on the passing flood.
   Or, if you would resist old Time's black hole,
   these windows of my eyes reflect your soul.

11

Look outward through the inward of my eyes
to see that self which never can decay,
reflected in the glass which never lies,
the gem that burns within the body's clay.
Your soul and mine unite beneath our skins
and intricately counterclockwise coil,
defying time and matter, fashions, sins,
mocking external lovers who embroil
their dying flesh in union's imitation,
their altogether in their all-in-all,
blunting their blades on stony limitation,
then whetting sharp to once more rise and fall.
    Your mirror shows you what will grace your tomb.
    My eyes show you which *you* escapes that doom.

12

How vainly I contest your vanity,
for, gazing in my eyes, you see no soul,
but faces like your own, as fresh and free,
golden and eager, fleshed out hale and whole.
Nor would I, had I wizard wit and tongue,
those sweet self-loving images dispel,
whose beauty I have worshipped and have sung,
regarding it, as you do, *non pareil*.
I would not blur my vision now, nor yours,
with tears that mourn what has not come to pass.
Let us be blind as careless paramours
who see no future in the gypsy glass.
    Our souls be damned. Our bodies here and now
    are fit not for the sickle, but the plough.

13

The weatherman predicts a gloomy front;
the almanac warns of a frigid fall;
the message of the calendar is blunt
and witnessed by the clock upon the wall.
Such signals vainly strain against a stronger:
the instant beauty in your mirror's gleam
which calls the future a mere gossipmonger
and scoffs at truth as nothing but a dream.
Of what may we avail ourselves while reason
is thus suspended, tangled in its laws?
While jester Now distracts the kingly Season,
may we not snatch our pleasure from his jaws?
   Oh, let us take advantage of Time's blunder
   and stretch an age betwixt the flash and thunder.

14

What eagles are we who can seize the day!
(We are but fledglings smothered in its grip.)
What asses dream that they control the dray,
as though there were no reins nor stinging whip.
The dense, heroic boulder braves the river,
ignoring how the water moulds the stone.
The bridegroom, seeing pink flesh all aquiver,
forgets that evening's bride is morning's crone.
I said your beauty's sure oblivion
was salvaged by your soul--a desperate lie.
To think yourself immortal, get a son,
and then, before he ages, quickly die.
   A photo fades, a statue crumbles, and
   this poem is a castle in the sand.

15

Nor soul nor son nor poem can endure
Time's sudden waves that treacherously race
into each inlet and each aperture
along broad beaches, leaving not a trace
of castles built with childish artistry
in momentary lapses of the tides.
Squealing we run before the swelling sea
and find blank margins when it next subsides.
And yet I leave my imprint on the sand,
printing in vain, in vain print print again,
till oceans cease their washing of the land
or Death shall, to my story, write Amen.
  So long as I have life and Time leaves spaces,
  I celebrate the beauty Time erases.

16

I celebrate the beauty Time erases
as old Cuchulain, swinging his steel sword,
slicing the water, buffeting its embraces,
alone against the surf so vainly warred.
Vain as a beauty captive in a tower
and languishing before the glass are you.
Vainly I go, thinking I serve this flower
performing futile feats of derring-do.
Thus love pursues its immemorial folly
and spins its filmy web to capture Time,
which crashes through in a relentless volley
and will not be ensnared by any rhyme.
  Yet as the green life force flings forth at Death,
  I sing your beauty till Time take my breath.

17

How restlessly I chide the one I cherish!
The future waits while I the present use
explaining to the blossom it will perish,
wasting the spring with this and other news.
Why can I not learn his sublime disdain,
relish the moment with which I am blessed,
and, to time's torrent, lift a brow urbane,
riding the river in apparent rest?
Who bears the fire gives thought to naught but burning,
but I am one who, by his beauty fired,
am constantly to a constant theme returning,
and for this restless mission am required:
    that those who cannot see the light may know
    and through these words discern its passing glow.

18

Shall I compare thee to thy Aston Martin?
Thou hast a quicker pick-up and ignition.
Oh, engineers are still in kindergarten
puzzled by the design of thy transmission.
Compared to thee, thy elegant *coupé*
might park in stables and subsist on silage.
Thy dash has dials in luminous array
recording greater speed and better mileage.
Not fuel injection, no, nor carburetor
could formulate that essence, sweet concoction,
that keeps thee running earlier and later
and longer, when thy heap has gone to auction.
    Thy beauty wrenches cannot make nor mar,
    and even sonnets may outlast thy car.

19

December winds are howling through the streets
ravaging all they find like Scythian hordes
and round the windows of our high retreats
sharpen themselves on stone like singing swords.
A war abroad, at home a murderous storm
sheeting the city in newspaper grey--
this night of dread commencing will perform
all horrors left undone this dreadful day.
But while these furies vainly scourge the planet
and Time unleashes her most deadly squall,
our love persists, as lichen grows on granite
beneath the torrent of the waterfall,
   such delicate life the waste of Time affords,
   which you inspire and my green verse records.

20

Old Chanticleer, feeling his oats this morning,
at crack of dawn to frosty barntop flew
and thought it right to give the farm fair warning,
but, oh, what can a cock-a-doodle do
but stand and crow and shake his scarlet head
and to the morning air make his proud point
if sleepers huddle sluggishly abed
and mutter that the cock is out-of-joint?
Truth is, I did steal one admiring glance,
then closed my eye and seemed to doze, in fear
of what next steps my waking might advance,
not knowing what to make of Chanticleer.
   My rooster, by a braver one reduced,
   hid his shy head in safety of the roost.

21

White lilies nod more beauteous on their stems,
I must confess, than my love napping lies,
and, at the jeweler's, I've seen brighter gems
than those that sparkle in his opening eyes.
Roses can make me swoon, but it's absurd
to claim that his scent gives me vertigo.
As for the music of his voice, I've heard
as good or better on the radio.
The qualities I love are truly his,
and rank embellishment would be uncouth.
His virtue is to be just what he is,
and mine, poetic license to speak truth.
    When poets dress their lovers up in lies
    one wonders why they have to advertise.

22

I saw an old man stare at me this morning
with sudsy beard across the bathroom sink,
a spectre sent by Time to give me warning
that I am aging faster than I think.
Swiftly I thought of you, and swift grew young,
watching the white beard gurgle down the drain.
What Time unravels can be newly strung
by a kind of knitting action of the brain:
I know my heart is yours, and think yours mine,
that we are one beneath our tents of skin,
and, bound more fastly than Time can untwine,
our souls are Siamese, cannot untwin.
    In you, my mirror, my own self I see,
    thinking till age catch you, it can't catch me.

(from the Rival Poet to the Young Man)

Nor lissome our light adagio, no, nor wrought
ponderously in taffeta sarabande,
but barbarously are we apache-caught
in slap of sweating skins, then madly flung
spinning from neon dreams, our flesh unwinding,
delirious as marbles spilled, our dance
blindly oracular, bulging, rending
the glacial silence with our avalanche.

And now this salty calm in twisted sheets,
dark languor, bobbing coals of cigarets,
we drift, lathed by the tide of soft regret . . .

but feel the gathering poison in our groins,
the scorch of lust, the appetite for pain,
and hear the gypsy fiddle wild disdain.

23

When I watch weary actors in rehearsal
with leaden voice mouth out their golden parts,
then give their tattered scripts a swift perusal,
and once more fail to give their words their hearts,
I think I have heard lovers' declarations,
recited like a part one mumbles through,
their affirmations coming out negations,
since feigning tones make truest words untrue.
In such a case, better to drop the curtain
and try the play again some other time,
or silence words of which one is uncertain
and act one's meaning out in graceful mime.
    I love to listen when your words are clear,
    but rather you be still than insincere.

24

With eye for lens and brain for film, my art
makes images upside down and black things white
until they are developed in my heart,
which turns them inside out and sets them right.
Your portrait hangs there, framed and rectified,
essence distilled, beyond all mortal change,
for though Time scratch and tear at your outside,
my inner image she'll not disarrange.
But will the world not thereby be deprived
of what my private archives hold unseen?
In future times, can beauty be revived
by some projection on a public screen?
    No flickering picture could present you fair,
    but words carve soul--which Time cannot impair.

25

If you were but an idiot, deaf and dumb,
devoid of reason as the beasts and birds,
unable to compute your fingers' sum,
you might believe I love you, not your words.
If garments come between us, cast them by.
I do not love a haberdasher's frill.
Your naked beauty gladdens every eye,
but were you ugly, I would love you still.
You think I love your name? Then nameless be.
You think I love your deeds? Then nothing do.
You think my love is based on yours for me?
Your hate could not shake my devotion true.
    Though I despair of language to convince,
    you are, when most a pauper, still my prince.

26

Odds are against us. Even if lovers find
their opposite number in the possible range,
and juices fuse inside the wiry mind
where signals pulse across the world's exchange,
they soon are disconnected. Though one goes
on shouting the empty line, flipping the book,
dialing the code again and again, he knows
that busy buzz means love is off the hook.
Yet I would slip my token in the slot
of this machine and finger out my choice
and think it lucky if at most I got
three minutes in the darkness of your voice,
    unraveling the automated gods,
    connecting mind with mind against the odds.

27

As magnets act through substances and space,
exerting force the subtlest cannot see,
so, though I dare not show you now my face,
your field's invisible authority
draws filaments of mind in patterns strange,
and these words flow in one direction true
toward that motive pole that sets my range.
They point like compass needles straight to you.
But since I cannot come to where you stay
and whither you are pointed cannot tell,
I fear you may turn round the other way
and what you drew, with that same force repel.
    I spin confused in answer to your action,
    trusting I will be guided by attraction.

28

I close my eyes. The city sinks from sight
as though these stony canyons slipped beneath
the sea, and silt had settled white on white,
all life succumbing to night's closing teeth.
My head is like a winter landscape gleaming,
despite the darkness, filled with icy light.
Under sleep's snow the ghostly glow of dreaming
pulses, although all else is frozen tight.
What is that presence that persists in throbs
under the season's mantling chilly deep
that heat from winter, light from blackness robs?
What ghost disturbs my drifts of deathly sleep?
   You bring to my numb mind the force of life.
   You pale December's darkness, dull its knife.

29

When I have fallen through the film of dreams
and know I am alone in night's black grip,
the room with figures for my torment teems,
each with his gloating grin and special whip.
"How small his mind," says one, "its gift how dim."
Another says, "His flesh was misbegot."
A third says, "That would not disable him
were his heart generous. Alas, it's not."
I twist in sweaty sheets and stare again
while blackness batters me with truth on truth
and my lungs scream for some new oxygen
to leak into this sealed confession booth.
   I gasp one thought of you--that saving air:
   Breathing your love, I can these demons bear.

30

Bound as I am to suffer the parade
of jangled memories in *danse macabre,*
past beauty in grotesquery arrayed,
old loves in motley mocking from the mob,
lean Disappointment shaking his long scythe,
imagined Triumph crawling on the ground,
forgotten Pleasure wracked and doomed to writhe
along the route where I am witness-bound,
then my brow feels the grinding of a wheel
groaning along my nerves (those ancient ruts
first made by first experience) whose steel
in each return to mind more deeply cuts.
 Only your presence makes these tortures fade,
 shaming the Past and her absurd charade.

31

As a traveler who gathered on the road
mementoes from each place that he had been
until each step he struggled with the load
of he knew not what, nor why acquired, nor when,
so I collected curios of caring,
thinking I could contain all I had known,
till smothered by the rubbish I was bearing
and haunted by the ghosts I tried to own,
I found a love containing in his person
the essence of all other loves before,
whose presence made those ancient values worsen,
so that I cast them off and nothing wore
 except the radiance of all-in-one,
 whose touch is light and warming as the sun.

(the Young Man attempts a response)

You talk about casting off and wearing nothing,
but I know when I get there you'll be clothed,
and the very touch you claim you find so soothing
you'll reject in favor of things you claimed you loathed.
When I am gone you cannot do without me;
when I am there I find you can, in fact,
and though you say you love everything about me,
when challenged, you say, "Well, in the abstract."
So let me abstract be, your Big Idea,
and let me dwell at ease inside your head,
for which I can remain in Franconia,
and no question will arise about the bed.
    It's no fun being figment for a dreamer
    who makes you play both Sin and Sin's Redeemer!

32

Eat cotton candy flesh, and for blood's drink,

swill pink pop while his magic carousel
thumps *oom-pa-pa*. At such time should I think
water would interest you from my still well?

You may a geyser get, or the kitchen sink,
from fashion's shaman, whose sleek sleight-of-hand
whistles up swift symbolic rink-a-dink

so dazzling that you needn't understand,
and, if you drink not, may forget your thirst
chasing the gay mirage across the sand.

In midway ways I grant I'm poorly versed:
I stand, and nothing buy, and nothing sell,
and nothing say but what I said at first--

no style I know save that of loving well.

(the Dark Lady slips the Poet a note
on opening night of his first play)

I'm here as a reviewer for the *Voice,*
but I know I cannot say in my review
I think you're hauling coal in your Rolls Royce.
What interests me is not this play, but you.
Your slapstick dipped in honey, you flailed a warren
of rodent lovers romping routes well-known
around a plot derivative and foreign,
bouncing like marbles on a xylophone,
yet I heard through soft nonsense a hard tongue
that parried my critique and scored *touché,*
a mordant wit and eloquence which stung
and tingled like a vinegar douche. Say
   when we can meet and where we can together
   wipe off that slapstick and renew its leather.

33

After the howling night comes morning breaking,
spilling its stillness like a flood of gold,
exciting twittering birds to glad awaking
as shadows shrink and glittering shapes unfold.
We saunter shirtless forth and smile, unheeding
towering soft clouds gathering far away,
so thickly whitely innocently breeding
chill wind and rain that soon will black our day.
So gloried I in his forever dawning
and flittered in a greening world benign
until disfavor lowered like an awning,
slicing off light I thought was surely mine,
   yet I would rather have uncertain weather
   than be denied such radiance altogether.

34

A cur found by a child, loose in the street,
is sometimes taken up and bathed and fed,
given a name, spoiled with embraces sweet,
and soon forgets being mangy, starved, near dead,
but flicks across the child's attention span
like other pets, no doubt, and many a toy,
and then, neglected, feels more misery than
a dog that never did such love enjoy.
So was I found, named, coddled, nurtured, groomed,
and slept at hearthside in one's love secure,
but now to slink in alleys am I doomed,
and suffer what I once could well endure,
    for having learned such luxury to savor,
    I find all bleak beside his moment's favor.

35

This leaning ball that spins through frigid space
is held on course by forces none can see.
A grave pull sucks it to the sun's hot face,
but swinging impels toward empty liberty.
So would my binding urge have pulled us down
till we were buried in love's molten mass,
but your sprite, like a fleck from grindstone thrown,
flew out and cooled, escaping love's morass.
Oh vain analogy, that would excuse
your sparking traffic off to anywhere,
and vain, ingenious lover I, to use
such arguments my own heart's hurt to spare,
    for you have gone off rutting after action,
    and I spin similies for satisfaction.

36

What you have done or why I will not ask,
nor doubt your license to do it again.
One in our love, we wear a two-faced mask,
and neither knows the other's where or when.
To save that love, let's go our separate ways--
more social yours, more solitary mine--
which neither gossip nor presumption raise
and what they do not consummate, resign.
Dispassionately this contract I propose,
yet, when it comes to signing, shilly-shally,
remembering hours when minds curled in repose
and gazing soft was cause enough to dally.
    But, no, I must resist those thoughts' allure
    and hope by parting we may keep them pure.

37

A son outgrows his sweet dependency,
no longer holding his old man in awe,
and to affirm his manhood finally
finds that he must confront him, jaw to jaw;
and--since the father aged is, and weak,
and cannot win a showdown--if he's wise,
he'll ride his rising son's climb to the peak
and means to share that glory will devise.
So let me think your beauty, wealth and wit
are somehow mine and will, in age, sustain me,
and though it be demeaning, yet is fit
that I from seeking justice shall refrain me,
    and that your victory, though at my cost,
    somehow is mine, and thus is nothing lost.

38

That storm of fire, the silent sun, evokes
green swarming growth and mankind's grateful smiles
through winter's chill and summer's cloudy cloaks
across dead space of ninety million miles.
The secret atom's devastating power,
the germ of plague, and precious life's protein,
the seed that holds the formula of flower--
all work their influence unheard, unseen.
So though with sonic boom and jet stream blurring
you tilt away into a distant sky,
invisible beams of love pursue unerring:
You are not lonely, nor abandoned I,
    such signals pulse between us, dream to dream,
    and, wordless, give my words their constant theme.

39.

The world has come between us. Let us be
like those imaginary frozen poles
joined only by a fictive axletree
on which, supposedly, the whole ball rolls.
Geographers may calibrate their maps
with declinations from our fixed ideal.
Lest longitude and latitude collapse,
we should no closer be, nor no more real.
Discreetly may one love, a world away,
his other self, without such vanities
as those too close, too much alike, betray,
who cannot reach to strict antipodes.
    Let each then find his lone and steady station
    so love may bear this dizzy world's rotation.

40

My sulky angel, do you think you can,
by stealing one I love, become a thief?
Long since you conquered all my full heart's span,
and what you have not taken, hold in fief.
That guilt that sours your day and keeps you waking,
thinking that it was me whom you betrayed,
betrays you. What you took was yours for taking,
a crime that in my balance nothing weighed.
No thief are you, and yet to self a traitor,
deriding a mount you could not wait to ride,
then, gilding over that guilt with a greater,
to placate self abused, to self you lied.
   Angel of grace, teach me that treachery
   that blinds blind justice, sanctions lechery.

41

Our flesh can execute with a *carte-blanche*
the resolutions of mind's legislature,
but with no check from soul's judicial branch,
such action is mere will of savage nature.
Oh thrilling thrall, voluptuary will!
Oh, ill illusion, any Will above!
I hunger, too, and too soon have my fill,
and yet still crave the only Will I love.
I know the woman well who whispered, "Come,"
and well the Will that courteously followed,
and well the swing of that flesh pendulum
that swells the head and leaves the heart all hollowed,
   and know the junction of two I adore
   means all lose all in seeking more and more.

42

I hate you merely for the thing you are,
for essence, as opposed to means and ends.
Since we have her in common, on a par,
we are in principle foes, in function friends.
The hunchback and the athlete lie together
like lamb and lion, loving in the storm.
In this case she provides the pandar weather,
so come and cuddle up. My hunch is warm.
Ah, if virago Winter would continue,
our cave might stay as cozy as it should.
But I have pride, and you have glands within you.
One smile of Spring, and farewell brotherhood!
   Thus love that brings two leaping to be one
   forever leaves two other loves undone.

43

Her love for me, my love for you, will vanish
as glaciers do when gravely they descend,
and icy Latin melts to liquid Spanish,
and common source flows off to private end,
as waxen visage of a Catholic order
erupts in pimples of a Renaissance,
and fugitives leak through the Berlin border
to freedom *(honi soit qui mal y pense)*,
so will our Trinity, now fixed in truce,
burn, twirl, blur, fizzle, spend itself in faction,
when once she smiles, and you spring to her, loose,
and I watch Being fertilized by Action--
   huddled and hurt, sensuous from afar,
   and envy what you do, hate what you are.

128

Not *Kama Sutra* ecstasy I praise--
with one leg wound around your you-know-what,
nor ointments which a flaccid lingam raise
to grease the pivot of a yoni *(twat)*.
We tried all that: grunting the barbells up
while tightrope sauntering with feckless ease
before we swiveled round to *swive* or *tup*
swinging by knees aloft on a swift trapeze.
Diversity, a spice that jades the tongue,
forever adds to much too little more,
stringing one out until one is unstrung,
relieving boredom with new ways to bore.
    Now that extreme I seek is bedrock norm:
    the trackless freedom of our sonnet form.

138

I am not worthy of your love because
I think I am not worthy. You think you are
a creature crazed with webs of. secret flaws
who can be loved by no one on a par,
thus must deceive to hold. I think you lie
when you say I am worthier than I think,
yet since I think you worthier than I,
I love your lie as a thirsty man loves drink.
We would correct our faults, except they thrust
deeper than steamy fissures in the earth.
We would ignore them, but we cannot trust
that giddy love which is not based on worth,
    so when we lie together we lie asunder,
    and what our bodies know our minds still wonder.

(Sonnets 44-127, 129-137, and 139-154 have not been completed.)

I N D E X